Note to Readers

While the Allerton and Harrington families are fictional, the stock market crash of 1929 began one of the most difficult periods in American history, the Great Depression. At the worst part of the Depression, about one-third of America's workers were unemployed.

The teenager, June Kelly, was a real person who tried for the tree-sitting record in August 1930, just as it's described in this book.

Tuberculosis, or TB, was also very real. Throughout the beginning of this century, sanatoriums around the country were filled with TB patients hoping to regain their health.

Eventually better treatments and a better understanding of the disease made it almost disappear. But in recent years, drug-resistant forms of TB have surfaced, and it is once again becoming more common. Scientists and health professionals are working hard to keep TB from becoming as widespread as it once was.

The American Adventure

BLACK
TUESDAY

JoAnn A. Grote

BARBOUR
PUBLISHING, INC.
Uhrichsville, Ohio

Published by Barbour Publishing, Inc., P.O. Box 719, Uhrichsville, Ohio 44683
http://www.barbourbooks.com

ecpa Member of the
Evangelical Christian
Publishers Association

Printed in the United States of America.

Cover illustration by Peter Pagano.
Inside illustrations by Adam Wallenta.

CHAPTER 1

The Grand Opening

Fred Allerton felt a tug at his hat. "Hey!" He grabbed for the visor and held on tight. He scowled, his glance darting about the crowded hallway. Who had tried to grab his hat?

He caught sight of his father's black and gray hair. Mother stood beside him. Father's dark-eyed gaze fixed on Fred. Father held his own straw dress hat by its brim in one hand. He lifted it slightly, smiled, and winked.

Fred dragged his hat from his strawberry-blond hair. His cheeks felt hot. As usual, he'd forgotten to remove his hat when they entered the building. But it wasn't like it was a church or a home, he argued to himself. Any boy would forget a little thing like taking off his hat when he entered the tallest building west of Chicago!

Fred and his parents were carried along by the crowd toward the middle of the building.

"Oof!" Fred's eight-year-old cousin, Alice, fell against him. He helped her stand up. "Are you all right?"

Alice nodded, her short blond hair catching the light. "Yes. Somebody bumped me." She scowled down toward her feet. "They stepped on my new white shoes, too!"

Fred laughed. "My feet have been stepped on so much this afternoon that I'm beginning to think they're part of the floor. There must be twenty thousand people here."

Alice's eyes sparkled with a smile. "Isn't it exciting? I liked the church service." She fanned her face with her bulletin. All around them, others were doing the same. It was over ninety degrees, and there wasn't any room for a breeze in the crowded hallway. "Wasn't it fun to sing hymns with the band?"

"Sure was," Fred agreed. The band was still playing, even though the service was over. He could hear the music over the voices of the people crowding the hall.

"It's the John Phillip Sousa Band," their sixteen-year-old cousin Addy reminded them. "It's one of the most famous bands in the world." Her brown curls bobbed as she swung lightly to the music. Addy was quiet and shy, but she liked to dance.

Addy's father was a reporter for the Minneapolis *Tribune*. He was busy covering the opening of the building for a newspaper story. There were many people he had to talk to, so Addy and her mother were spending the afternoon with Fred and Alice's families.

Fred frowned and looked up at her. "Was that old man leading the band Mr. Sousa? The one wearing the coat with the big brass buttons?"

"Yes. He's seventy-five, but his band is very good, isn't it?" Addy asked.

"I liked their music," Fred said. "I've never been to a church service where we had to stand in the street before, though. Or where both a Methodist minister and a Jewish rabbi spoke and prayed."

Addy started to say something then began coughing, covering her mouth with her white gloved fingers.

"Are you all right?" Alice asked when Addy stopped coughing.

Addy smiled down at her while pulling a white handkerchief from her skirt pocket. "Yes. I just have a little cold."

The crowd surged forward again. Fred grabbed Alice's hand so she wouldn't get pushed off her feet again.

They came to a stop in the hallway by the elevators with their marble doors. They watched as people came off the elevators. Then they were caught up again as a wave of people tried to get into the elevators.

"Guess we'll have to wait for the next one," Fred said as the elevator doors slid shut.

"Look!" Alice pointed behind him. "There's the statue of George Washington."

Fred turned around. Sure enough, there was a statue of the head and shoulders of the first president of the United States. "I hear Mr. Foshay spent lots of money to have a famous sculptor make that."

"The bishop today said Mr. Foshay wants the statue to remind people that this tower was built in memory of George Washington," Alice said, "because Mr. Foshay thinks he was such a good man."

The building was even built to look a bit like the Washington Monument in Washington, D.C. Its walls sloped from the larger bottom walls to the narrower ones on top.

The elevator doors opened, people came out, and finally

Alice and Fred and their families entered. Fred could hardly contain his excitement. He grinned at his older cousin Addy Moe. "Only a couple minutes, and we'll be at the top of the tallest building between here and the Pacific Ocean!"

The uniformed elevator boy shut the marble doors and started the elevator. Fred's stomach seemed to turn over as the elevator started up at what seemed a terrific speed.

While the elevator was moving, the elevator operator spoke to the people in the car. The boy looked to Fred to be no more than eighteen. His chin was lifted proudly, and he spoke in a crisp, businesslike voice. "The Foshay Tower is twenty-two stories high. It's the tallest building this side of Chicago. Construction began two years ago, in 1927. On weekdays, business offices fill the floors we're passing.

"When you entered the elevator," he continued, "you probably noticed the button beside the door. It's the newest thing for elevators. When a person on any floor wants to enter the elevator, all they need do is push the button. The elevator will then stop at the floor automatically. The person doesn't need to worry the elevator operator will miss the old-fashioned blinking light and forget to stop at his floor!"

The boy flashed a grin at the people crowded into the elevator, and they all grinned back at him. Fred didn't think this sharp-minded boy would ever forget his duties.

The elevator stopped, and the boy opened the heavy doors. "This is the observation deck. You're four hundred feet high here, folks! Enjoy the view."

"Four hundred feet!" Alice's brown eyes were wide as they left the elevator. "I bet we'll be able to see forever, maybe as far as the Rocky Mountains!"

Fred laughed and shook his head, then put his hat back on.

"We won't be able to see that far. Most of Minnesota, all of South Dakota, and most of Wyoming are between us and the Rockies."

"But this is the highest building between here and the mountains," Alice reminded him.

The crowd of people moved as close to the railing as possible, pushing Alice and Fred along with them. The two cousins pressed against the railing, peering over the top. Fred noticed that even standing on tiptoe in her new shoes, Alice couldn't look over the railing and straight down. She was only a little taller than the railing was high.

"The railing is too tall," she complained to Fred.

"That's why your brothers and sister had to stay downstairs with your mother," Fred told her. "Most children aren't tall enough to see over the railing until they're eight."

All around them, people were saying, "Ooh!" and "Aah!" and "I've never seen anything like it!"

"It's like being in the clouds, isn't it?" Addy asked.

Fred and Alice glanced up at her. Addy had one hand on the railing. Her other gloved hand was holding her hat so it wouldn't blow off.

Fred yanked his hat down tighter over his hair, too. "Quite a breeze up here," he said. Then he smiled. "Feels good, though. It's awfully hot today. Glad I only had to wear my good white shirt and brown shorts and not a suit like Father is wearing."

"The breeze does feel good," Alice agreed. Her yellow linen dress stuck to her because of the heat.

Addy coughed again. When she was done, Alice said, "Maybe you shouldn't be in this wind with your cold."

Addy smiled at her. "I'm fine, but thank you for caring."

Fred's older brother Harry grinned, his brown eyes

9

sparkling with excitement. "The only time I've been higher than this is in an airplane."

Alice's brow wrinkled in a frown. "Do you think airplanes will hit the tower? It's awfully high. What if they don't see it in the dark?"

"They won't be able to miss seeing it." Harry pointed to the part of the tower that rose above them. "There are two large beacon lights up there. One of them turns, shining its light all over the city. Pilots will use it to help them know where they are when they fly at night."

Alice bent her head way back to stare up at the pointed top of the building. "I bet the airmail pilots that fly at night will be glad for that light."

The new night airmail service between Minneapolis and Chicago had only begun a month ago.

"I'm sure you're right," Harry agreed.

Fred grinned. "I think Colonel Lindbergh wishes he could see a beacon light on his flight."

"Why?" Alice asked.

"He and his wife are flying over one thousand miles of the Amazon jungle in South America this weekend. They are flying the first United States mail service from Miami, Florida, to Dutch Guiana."

"Is that dangerous?" Alice asked.

"Dangerous?" Fred's eyebrows slid up out of sight beneath his hat's visor. "I'll say it's dangerous! There aren't any maps of the Amazon jungle. If the Lindberghs' plane crashed, they might never be found."

A shiver ran down Alice's spine. "Lost in a jungle! It sounds like the title of a movie serial instead of something that could happen to a nice man like Colonel Lindbergh."

"Lindbergh will make it through safe. You'll see." Harry's voice sounded sure.

"But there are reports of plane crashes in the news every day," Alice told him.

"Not Lindbergh's plane," Harry assured her. "He's a good pilot. He's not going to crash."

"Harry should know," Fred told her. "He met Lucky Lindy, you know."

"I suppose you're right," Alice said, "but I still worry about Colonel Lindbergh and his pretty wife. The idea of being lost in a jungle is frightening."

Addy held onto her hat with one hand and bent her head back, looking at the top of the tower. "Didn't one of the speakers mention the beacon lights today? They said something about the lights being a shining reminder of the light God put inside people, the light George Washington called conscience."

"That's right," Harry said.

The deck went all around the tower. The cousins and their families moved to another side of the deck. They wanted to see the city from every side. Fred's father pointed out different well-known spots to Fred and Alice: Dayton's department store, the flour mills, even the Mississippi River and the huge bridges that crossed it.

Alice's hands clutched the railing as her gaze followed his pointing finger. "Everything looks so small! The flour mills always looked so high to me from the ground."

"They don't look as small as the people and cars on the street below." Fred was looking over the side.

Their families moved on to the next side of the tower, but Alice and Fred stayed behind for a minute.

Alice stood on tiptoe and stretched her neck as far as she

11

could, but she still couldn't bend her head to look over the railing at the sidewalk beside the building.

"Hi, Alice!"

Alice dropped back down on her heels and turned in surprise at her school friend's voice. "Dot!"

Dorothy Lane, or Dot as everyone called her, was wearing one of the prettiest dresses to be seen that day. It was a sleeveless white silk with a huge blue satin bow tied at the drop waist. A matching tall white straw hat with a tiny brim and a blue satin ribbon kept her short, dark red hair from tossing in the wind the way Alice's blond hair was doing.

"Hi, Dot," Fred said. "I didn't know you'd be here."

"I had to be here." Dot lifted her pointed chin. "My father is an important man in Mr. Foshay's company. He has a beautiful office in the tower, you know."

"Oh, that's nice." Fred saw Alice smile out of the corner of his eye. He knew she liked it when he acted like he'd never heard of Mr. Lane's job before. Dot had been telling all their friends for months how important Mr. Foshay thought her father was and how much money her father made.

Dot moved to the railing between Alice and Fred. She grinned at them. "Did you know Mr. Foshay paid John Phillip Sousa twenty thousand dollars to play this weekend? Mr. Foshay tied the check to something heavy enough not to float away. Then he dropped it over the side of the railing to where Mr. Sousa stood on the sidewalk below."

Fred and Alice laughed.

Dot pointed a finger in a white cotton glove over Alice's shoulder. "Look at that man in the jacket with the torn pocket and the patched trousers."

"Shhh! He'll hear you!"

12

"I don't care if he hears me. I don't think the guards should have let people come up here who aren't dressed well."

"Maybe the man is poor and those are the best clothes he has," Alice said softly.

Dot crossed her arms. "Then he shouldn't be here. This is an important day. People should be dressed up."

Fred noticed how red Alice's cheeks grew at her friend's tone. He couldn't blame her. Dot was being downright rude.

"I don't think George Washington would mind the way that man's dressed," Fred said in a friendly voice, "and after all, the building was built to remind people of George Washington and what a good man he was, wasn't it?"

For once, Dot was silenced. Fred basked in Alice's grateful smile. He was glad he'd been able to stop Dot's nasty words without saying anything mean.

Alice and Fred's families came up behind Fred. "Are you two ready to go?" Alice's father asked.

Fred and Alice said good-bye to Dot and started toward the elevator door with the others. They walked beside Addy. The three of them were behind the rest of their families. Addy was walking slowly, but Fred and Alice didn't mind.

"I hate to leave, don't you?" Alice asked Addy.

Addy didn't answer.

Fred felt Addy's hand on his shoulder. He looked up at her. Addy stopped walking. Her cheeks were very red. Something about the way she looked made Fred's stomach feel funny. "Is something wrong, Addy?"

"I. . .I don't feel very good. I think I. . .I might. . ."

Addy's eyes closed. She leaned hard on Fred's shoulder. Alice reached out both hands to help her. Then Addy started to fall.

13

CHAPTER 2

What's Wrong with Addy?

Terror flooded Alice. "Help! Father, help!"

She couldn't take time to see whether Father had heard her. She struggled to hold Addy, but Addy was too heavy. Even with Fred's assistance, she couldn't hold Addy up. Alice's knees buckled, and she sat down heavily on the stone floor with a grunt. Her arms were still around Addy.

Addy's eyes were closed. "Addy, wake up!"

"Addy!" Addy's mother, Aunt Esther, dropped to her knees beside the three cousins. She reached for one of Addy's gloved hands.

Alice could hear the fright in Aunt Esther's voice. It made the fear inside her grow stronger.

Fred's father, a doctor, knelt on the other side of Addy. He took her wrist in his hand. Pushing back the top of her short white gloves, he felt for her pulse.

"Is she all right?" Aunt Esther asked him.

Uncle Richard frowned, still feeling for the pulse.

What happened to her? Alice wondered. *She has to be all right. She just has to! Please, God, make her all right.*

People stood about them, murmuring among themselves, watching Addy and Uncle Richard with curious eyes. They blocked out the breeze.

"Please stand back and let the girl get some air," Alice's father said. He made waving movements with his hands. The crowd moved back, but only a little.

Addy moaned. Her head rolled to one side, then the other. She opened her eyes and squinted against the sunlight.

"Addy!" Relief rushed through Alice.

"Addy!" her mother cried.

Addy frowned up at them. "What. . .what happened?"

"You fainted," Uncle Richard told her, letting go of her wrist.

"Fainted?" Addy blocked the sun out of her eyes with her hand. When she saw all the people standing about watching her, her cheeks grew red. She started to sit up, coughing.

Alice felt sorry for her. She knew Addy was embarrassed. She didn't like having strangers watch her. But Alice was more worried about Addy than anything else.

Uncle Richard stopped Addy with a hand against her shoulder. "Don't stand up yet. Take a minute to get your strength back."

15

The crowd about them began moving away, now that they could see Addy was okay.

"Are you feeling all right?" Aunt Esther asked, still holding one of Addy's hands. "I should never have let you come today. I should have made you stay at home in bed with that awful cold."

Addy gave her a small smile. "I'm all right, Mother. And I'm glad I came. I wouldn't have wanted to miss such an exciting day because of a silly cold."

Alice didn't blame her. She wouldn't have wanted to be home sick either when so many important people came to town. There were governors from other states here and the John Phillip Sousa Band. The president of the United States even sent a man to represent him. People had come from all over the world to see the opening of the Foshay Tower.

Uncle Richard was still frowning. He felt Addy's forehead and her flushed cheeks. "The combination of your cold and this heat might be the reason you fainted."

"Of course it is." Addy coughed again. "I'll be fine, Uncle Richard."

Uncle Richard stood up and helped Addy to her feet. "We'll find a water fountain downstairs," he told her. "Then we're taking you straight home, young lady. When you get there, I want you to go right to bed."

Alice scrambled up, too, brushing at the skirt of her yellow dress.

"Do you think she'll be all right?" Aunt Esther asked in a worried voice.

"I'm sure she will," Uncle Richard said, "as soon as she gets out of this heat. Give her some aspirin and lots of liquids and keep her in bed until this heat wave is over."

16

"I will."

Alice and Fred walked together, following the others to the elevator. Alice felt much better knowing it had only been a bad cold and the heat that had made Addy faint.

She turned for one last look. She couldn't see anything past the edge of the observation deck except sky. A smile slipped across her face. It was like Addy had said, like being in the clouds.

Two days later on the first day of school, Alice thought of Addy. It had been hot yesterday, over ninety degrees, and it was supposed to be just as hot today. She was glad she didn't have to stay in bed all day like Addy.

"Wish we didn't have to go to school today," Fred grumbled as they climbed the steep concrete stairs to the schoolhouse. "I'd rather be at one of the lakes, swimming."

Alice grinned. "Me, too. Let's ask our mothers to take us to the beach for a picnic for supper."

Fred's face brightened. "Good idea."

Alice hoped their mothers would take them to the beach later, but she was glad to be in school again, too. It was fun to see the friends she hadn't seen since last spring. It was hard to settle down and pay attention in class. She and her friends wanted to visit.

Alice was happy to see Dot was in her class. Their desks were right across the aisle from each other.

"I like your dress, Dot," she said.

Dot was wearing a pretty green silk dress with short sleeves, a dropped waist, and a short pleated skirt. The color of the dress matched the color of her eyes.

"Thank you." Dot played with the red hair that curled

perfectly against her cheek. "Mother says it's very fashionable. Your dress isn't, though, is it? It looks like a little girl's dress."

"It does not!" Alice's eyes hurt with sudden tears. She blinked them back.

The teacher told everyone to take their seats. Alice's chest still hurt from Dot's words when she sat down. She was wearing a brand new dress. Mother had taken her shopping at Dayton's for it. She'd chosen it special to wear the first day of school. She loved the pretty blue color and the wide white collar that came almost to her shoulders. She'd been so excited to wear it. And now Dot had spoiled it.

One of her first assignments was to write a short essay. Alice liked writing better than some of her other classes, but she'd rather have been telling her friends about her summer than writing about it for the teacher, Mrs. Sims.

Mrs. Sims was tall and skinny with short, dark, wavy hair parted on the side. She had a skinny face and wore glasses at the top of her straight, skinny nose.

Alice chewed on the end of her pencil for a few minutes, trying to decide what to write. Then she bent over her paper and printed her essay as carefully as she could, hoping she spelled all the words right.

After the writing assignment was over and the papers were passed to the front, Mrs. Sims passed out the social studies books. On the front of the book was a picture of a girl and boy about Alice's age. They were walking past a store.

"This year in social studies," Mrs. Sims told them, "we're going to study how cities grow and work and how people live in cities. That's what we'll learn about in this book. But next week we will have a special social studies week: the week of the United States Constitution. Does anyone know what the Constitution is?"

Some of the students raised their hands but not Alice. She'd heard of the Constitution, but she didn't really know what it was.

Mrs. Sims called on Dot.

Dot stood beside her desk the way all the students did when they were called on. "It's the rules that tell how the United States will be run."

Mrs. Sims nodded. "That's right."

With a pleased smile, Dot took her seat.

"Next week," Mrs. Sims continued, "all the classes in all the schools in Minneapolis will study the Constitution. It's important that everyone know how our government works. How many of you went to the Foshay Tower this weekend?"

Almost everyone in the class raised their hands.

Mrs. Sims nodded. "Good. Mr. Foshay built that tower to remind people of George Washington, our first president. James Madison and Alexander Hamilton wrote the words of the Constitution, but George Washington was one of the men who voted to make the Constitution the most important law in the United States."

Alice wished she knew more about George Washington, the first president of the United States. People had been talking about him all weekend. Mr. Foshay had built the Foshay Tower because he admired President Washington so much, even though President Washington lived over a hundred years ago. The only things Alice knew about him were that he was the first president and that when he was a boy, he didn't lie about cutting down a cherry tree. But she thought he must have been a wonderful man for people to think he was so important such a long time after he died.

She forgot about him, though, as soon as class was over. She and her friends hurried to the cafeteria, where they could finally talk to each other over lunch.

At the table, Alice made sure she didn't sit beside Dot. She still hurt from Dot's unkind words about her dress. She and her friends took their lunches out of their bags. They were almost too busy talking to eat.

Soon, Dot started talking about her father and the Foshay Tower again. The rest of the girls stopped talking to listen. Suddenly Dot leaned forward. In a loud whisper, she said, "Here comes Inez. Let's pretend we don't see her. We don't want her to eat with us."

"Why?" Alice stared at Dot in surprise.

Dot shrugged. "She isn't quite like the rest of us. Can't you tell? Her family doesn't have very much money, you know." She glanced toward Inez. "She's almost here. Pretend we don't see her."

Dot started telling the story of Mr. Foshay dropping the check off the observation deck. All the girls but Alice leaned forward, listening to Dot and laughing.

Inez stopped beside Alice. "Hi, Alice. I like your pretty dress."

"Thank you." Alice smiled at her.

The rest of the girls didn't even look at Inez.

Inez looked puzzled. Alice watched her round face as Inez's gaze swept the table. "I guess there isn't any place left to sit at this table."

Alice's cheeks grew hot. She wanted to ask Inez to bring a chair from another table and sit beside her, but she couldn't get the words out. Dot and the other girls would be angry with her if she asked Inez to sit with them.

"See you later, Alice." Inez walked to another table and sat down by herself with her back to Alice and her friends.

The other girls broke into a fit of giggles. Alice wasn't sure whether they were laughing at Inez or at Dot's story. Slowly, she put the rest of her sandwich back in her bag. Alice wasn't hungry anymore. Her stomach felt funny.

CHAPTER 3

The Crash

Alice jumped behind a tree just in time to miss the small snow-ball whizzing past. "You missed me!"

"I'll get you this time!" Fred raced toward the tree.

Alice fled through the front gate. Fred hurled another snowball at his cousin. It whipped over her head just as she ducked below the fence.

Fred smiled. Now he knew just how to get her. He slipped around the edge of the yard to a tree growing near the fence. Looking over, he spied Alice hurriedly pushing snow from the

22

ground beside her into a ball. She glanced through the slats of the white wooden fence, looking for him.

It was getting dark out, so Fred knew Alice would have a hard time seeing him standing against the dark tree trunk. She stood up slowly.

Whop! Fred's carefully aimed snowball hit her in the shoulder, making a white blotch against her red jacket.

"Gotcha!" Fred jumped out from behind the tree, a grin spread over his face.

Alice tossed her snowball at him. He threw himself to the ground to miss being hit. Then he laid on his back and threw his arms out. "I'm tired. Let's go inside. It must be almost time for *Amos and Andy* on the radio."

"Okay." Alice brushed the snow from her jacket as she came back into the yard. "Do you think we'll get much more snow?"

"Naw." Fred stood up and brushed leaves and snow from his own jacket and trousers. "It's only two days before Halloween. Dad says most of the snow's going to melt right away."

Alice wished the snow would last a while longer. She liked playing in it, and the world looked clean and new covered with snow.

When they went inside, Fred said, "Let's see if we can go to the movies Saturday. There's a new movie called *Coconuts* with the Marx Brothers. It's supposed to be really funny."

They stamped their feet on the rug inside the door to get the snow off their boots.

"Quiet!" Fred's father called from the living room. "We're trying to hear the news."

Fred pulled off his boots. "Shucks. We must have missed *Amos and Andy.*"

He and Alice walked into the living room. The adults were

23

all leaning forward in their chairs, looking at the brown radio as if they could see the man speaking.

On the rug in the middle of the floor, Alice's seven-year-old brother Steven was reading a Big Little Book while her five-year-old sister Isabel was playing quietly with a doll. Although Fred wasn't surprised to see quiet, serious Steven reading, he did think it odd that Isabel was being so quiet. She hardly ever sat still for more than a minute or two at a time.

Fred glanced at Alice. She was frowning at the people in the room. He could tell that she thought something seemed strange, too.

"What's going on?" Fred asked.

"Sh." His father held a finger to his lips.

Fred and Alice sat down cross-legged beside Steven and Isabel.

"Today," the news announcer was saying, "will be known as Black Tuesday for a long time to come. October 29, 1929, is indeed a dark day in America's history."

"Black Tuesday?" Alice asked.

"Sh!" This time it was Alice's mother shushing her.

Alice and Fred waited impatiently for the news program to end. Fred had been glad when his parents invited Alice's family and the Moes over for dinner. With being the youngest in his family and Harry being six years older, there was never anyone to play with at home.

But he didn't feel like playing now. The way the adults were acting made Fred's stomach feel funny. Something was wrong.

It seemed a long time to Fred before his father turned the radio off, the knob making a soft click. With a sigh, his mother leaned back in her rocker.

24

"Why is today Black Tuesday?" Alice asked right away.

"The stock market crashed," her father answered, running a hand through his dark, curly hair.

"I'm confused," Fred said. "I thought it crashed last week."

"Last Thursday was a very bad day for the stock market," his father agreed, "but today was the worst day ever."

Last week, Fred remembered, there had been reports that lots of men lost so much money on Thursday that they had killed themselves. Later news reports said it was only a rumor and people weren't jumping out of windows because they had gone broke.

Alice shook her head. "I don't understand. What *is* the stock market, anyway? Is it like a grocery market?"

The adults all laughed at Alice's question. Fred thought Alice looked embarrassed, but he was glad to see laughter on the adults' faces instead of the frowns they'd worn during the news.

"It *is* like a grocery market in a way," Alice's father told her. "At the stock market, people don't sell and buy groceries. They sell and buy pieces of companies instead. That's what a 'stock' is: a piece of a company."

Alice held out her hands, palms up. "How does a piece of a company crash? Did the walls fall down?"

Again the adults chuckled.

"No." Her father shook his head. "If the price of a stock is high, that usually means either the company is making a lot of money or people think the company *will* make a lot of money. If a company makes a lot of money, the people who own the stock make money."

"I still don't understand what crashed," Alice said.

Her father rested his elbows on his knees and leaned forward. "The cost of the stock crashed. That means the price of

25

a piece of a company went from a high price to a low price."

"And that's bad?" Fred asked.

"Sometimes yes and sometimes no," his father answered. "This time it looks pretty bad because the price of most of the companies sold on the stock market went down. That means people lost money."

Fred frowned. "I don't understand."

"Well, it's like this," his father said. "If I had bought a piece of the flour mill where Alice's father works, I would have paid money for stock in the company."

Fred nodded. So did Alice.

"Let's pretend I paid one hundred dollars for a piece of the flour mill. When the stock market crashed, the amount of money people would pay for a piece of the flour mill went down. Now I might only be able to sell the piece of the company I bought for twenty-five dollars. One hundred less twenty-five is seventy-five, so I've lost seventy-five dollars because now no one will pay one hundred dollars for my piece of the company."

"Oh. I think I understand now," Fred said. "A little, anyway."

Alice's forehead was puckered in a frown. "Did you lose lots of money on Father's company, Uncle Richard?"

Fred's father grinned and shook his head. "No, I don't really own stock in the mill."

"Oh." She was still frowning. "Is the company you work for going broke, Father?"

"No. Your uncle Richard only used my company for an example."

Alice breathed a loud sigh of relief. "Good. I'm glad you don't own any pieces of companies, Father."

"I own some but not very much. So does Uncle Richard.

But we don't own enough to worry about it."

"That's right," Fred's father agreed. "Don't you two worry about it. A lot of people are losing a lot of money because of the stock market crash, but most of them are wealthy people from the East."

"Like millionaires in New York City?" Fred asked.

His father nodded. "That's right. Not many people out here will be hurt by the crash."

Five-year-old Isabel got up from the floor and leaned against her mother's knee, her doll under one arm. "I'm tired of being quiet. Can I play loud now?"

Laughter filled the living room.

A moment later, Fred and Alice's mothers, Aunt Esther, and Alice were all on the floor playing with Isabel. Steven still had his nose in his book. Fred's father had turned the radio back on, and the men were trying to decide what program to listen to.

Everything looked happy. But an uncomfortable feeling was winding through Fred's chest.

If Father and Uncle Donald and Uncle Erik didn't lose money in the stock market crash, Fred thought, *why did they all look so worried during the news report?*

CHAPTER 4

Troublemakers

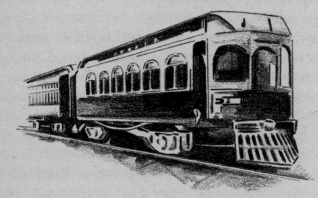

Two nights later on Halloween, Fred heard the news from the radio while he dressed in his costume.

"John D. Morgan has saved the stock market!" the reporter announced. "He has gathered a group of the wealthiest, most powerful businessmen in the country to buy stocks. Men like John D. Rockefeller Sr. They've put their money to good use in stopping the drop in the cost of stock."

Good! Fred thought, tying a red handkerchief around his

head like he'd seen pirates wear them in the movies. *Maybe now Father won't look so worried when he listens to the news.*

He picked up a chunk of coal and rubbed it above his top lip. Then he stood back and looked in the mirror. Not too bad. It didn't look like a real mustache, but it would look better outside in the dark. Now for the last piece.

He picked up a red crayon and drew a jagged line over his cheek. He grinned at his reflection in the mirror. "Can't be a pirate without a scar."

Before he left, he put on his winter jacket. Then he grabbed a piece of rope and used it to tie on a wooden sword he'd put together from scrap wood. He wished it weren't so cold. It was too cold to go out without his winter jacket, so the sword had to be tied around it.

Fred went into the living room to show his parents his costume before he left. While he was there, the reporter on the radio announced the news that a man in Kansas City had shot himself because of the stock market crash.

Fred hurried over to Alice's house. He and Alice had promised her mother that they'd take Steven and Isabel trick-or-treating. Fred's aunt opened the door with a loud "Meow!" Fred laughed when he saw her. She had pinned two pointed pieces of black velvet that looked like cat's ears to her hair. Black whiskers were drawn on her face. In her hand was the end of a black cord she'd tied about her waist. He could see it was supposed to be a cat's tail.

"Hello, Aunt Lydia."

Aunt Lydia slapped a hand to her chest and gasped. "A pirate! You look mighty fierce, Fred. I certainly wouldn't want to meet up with you on the high seas."

He grinned.

Aunt Lydia leaned closer to look at his face. "The scar is a great touch."

He was glad she appreciated his trouble. "I like your cat costume, too."

A group of children was hurrying up the walk, so Fred slipped into the hallway and let Aunt Lydia give them candy from the large bowl of homemade taffy she had on a table beside the door. A minute later, Alice, Steven, and Isabel joined him.

"We're almost ready," Alice told Fred. "Since Mother is watching the front door, I had to finish getting Isabel ready."

Isabel's brown eyes sparkled. "Look at me! I'm a kitty!"

"I can see that." Fred couldn't help but grin at her. She was wearing a warm cap that tied beneath her chin. Black velvet cat ears like the ones Aunt Lydia was wearing were pinned to the cap. Whiskers were drawn on her chubby cheeks.

"How are you going to say trick-or-treat if you're a cat?" he asked while Alice buttoned Isabel's wool coat.

"Me-ow!" Isabel said.

"Hold still while I pin on your tail," Alice told her.

Isabel tried to look over her shoulder at the tail while Alice pinned it on. Steven watched quietly. It didn't look to Fred like he was wearing a costume. "What are you tonight?"

"I'm a mill worker," Steven told him in his quiet voice. He held up a small, covered tin pail. "This is my lunch bucket. I was going to be an Indian. I even had a pheasant feather to use, but I didn't like the way it looked wearing my hat. And it's too cold not to wear a hat tonight."

"You're right. A mill worker was a good idea."

Steven smiled.

Alice finally got the tail pinned and stood up. She already

had on her coat. Over it she'd tied a large apron of her mother's. Fred could see it was pinned at her waist so it wouldn't drag on the ground. A large scarf was tied over her head.

"I'm a maid," she announced. She picked up a large tin pail like the ones maids and janitors used for water when they scrubbed floors. "I was going to bring a broom, but then I thought this pail would be easier to carry—and I can put my candy in it, too."

"Good idea," Fred approved.

Fred and Alice's parents didn't let them wear costumes of witches or ghosts or vampires like some kids wore. Their parents thought it was fun for the children to dress up and go trick-or-treating, but they didn't like them to wear costumes of evil or supernatural creatures. They weren't allowed to go to haunted house parties, either.

Although it was just turning dark outside, the sidewalks were filled with children in coats and costumes. Laughter and chatter and shrieks filled the air as they scurried about.

"Don't try that place. They make you do a trick before they give you a treat," Fred heard someone say.

Another trick-or-treater pointed to a large brick house across the way. "Don't miss their place. They have popcorn balls."

Candlelight shone from the cut-out faces of pumpkins of every shape and size on porches and steps and in windows. A light dusting of snow stuck to the ground, but it wasn't thick enough to hide the smell of dry autumn leaves.

Fred liked the excitement of Halloween. Even the cold air that stung his nose when he breathed didn't dampen his excitement. Just walking down the street made his heart beat faster. But his feet weren't moving as fast as usual. He and Alice and Steven all walked slowly to keep up with Isabel.

31

Isabel not only walked slowly, but she stopped often. She stared, wide-eyed, at the many costumed children who passed by. But once she learned that when she knocked on doors she received treats, she walked a little faster and stopped less often.

When they had gone up one side of the block and down the opposite side of the street, they took Isabel home, as they'd promised Aunt Lydia. Isabel was too young to go any farther, Aunt Lydia said.

The little girl was too excited showing her mother all the treats she'd collected to notice the other children leave again.

Since they'd already gone to all the houses in the block, the cousins headed farther out. Groups of other children still roamed the sidewalks, calling to friends they recognized.

A few blocks away from Alice's house, Fred began to see groups of older boys. Some were wearing masks and some weren't. Fred was pretty sure these boys were more likely to be playing tricks on people than they were to be collecting treats. His brother, Harry, had warned him to watch out for such boys. "Pranksters," Harry had called them. "Their tricks aren't always funny."

The three cousins started up the sidewalk to a corner house. "What!" Fred stopped so suddenly that Steven bumped into him.

"Why did you stop?" Alice asked.

Fred pointed to the front of the house. "There aren't any steps. They've been moved."

Wooden steps that should have been attached to the porch sat in the middle of the front lawn, leading nowhere. On the porch where the steps should have led, a pumpkin grinned out at them.

32

The children moved on to the next house. The steps hadn't been moved there, but a pumpkin was smashed on the sidewalk.

"Why do some people have to ruin things," Alice asked, "instead of just having fun? Why would they wreck things that belong to people who are nice enough to give them treats if they ask?"

Fred shook his head. "Guess they never heard of the Golden Rule: Do unto others as you would have them do unto you."

When they reached the street corner, Fred had to change his mind about where they would go next. Someone had opened the fire hydrant, and water was flooding the street.

"The street will be like an ice rink in the morning," he told Alice and Steven.

"Hey, look!" Steven pointed at the sky. A beam of light was moving across it. "What's that?"

"Wow! That must be from the light on top of the Foshay Tower," Fred told him.

"That's the light they said would remind people of George Washington and the conscience God put inside each of us," Alice said, staring at the beam that swept above them.

"It sure hasn't reminded some people," Fred said with a last glance at the water around the fire hydrant.

Halfway down the next block, Fred could see a big pile in the street.

"It looks like fence posts," Alice said.

"I think it is," Fred agreed. "Someone isn't going to be happy in the morning. I hope no one tears down our fence."

Someone was going to have to pull the fence out of the street before cars could drive by. Fred wondered if the fence posts were ruined or if the owner would be able to put them back up.

A shiver ran down Fred's spine. *Are the pranksters hiding nearby?* he wondered.

He looked around to see if whoever had piled the fence in the road was still around. He tried to act normal, not wanting to frighten Alice and Steven. As the oldest, he was in charge. He knew his parents and his aunt and uncle all expected him to watch out for Alice and Steven tonight.

All the damage seemed to take some of the fun out of the evening. Alice and Steven were quiet as they walked along. They still met some other trick-or-treaters but not as many. The other groups of kids weren't as noisy and full of laughter as the groups they'd met earlier.

Which is the safest way to go next? Fred wondered.

There was a trolley car stop at the next corner, and Fred headed toward it. "There should be more adults around there," he told Alice and Steven, "and street lights. I don't think any-one would dare wreck anything in such a public spot."

When they reached the corner, the trolley was at the stop. It was filled with people, but it wasn't going anywhere. The trolley driver in his brass-buttoned coat and visored hat was pushing a car off the tracks in front of the trolley. Two men in winter coats and galoshes were helping him.

"Why isn't there a driver in the car?" Steven asked.

"I don't think the owner knows his car is on the trolley tracks," Fred answered. "Would you park a car on the tracks?"

"No!" Steven shook his head back and forth fast. "The trolley might hit the car and wreck it."

"That's right. I think some big boys put the car on the tracks as a trick."

"That was mean."

"You're right, Steven," Alice agreed.

Fred nodded.

The three cousins had forgotten all about trick-or-treating. They watched the grunting men push the car past the edge of the tracks that ran down the middle of the street and leave the car beside the curb. The two men helping the trolley driver climbed into the trolley. The driver started to enter the trolley, too. Then he spotted Fred, Alice, and Steven.

A moment later he was striding toward them. He was still breathing hard from pushing the car. Little clouds formed in front of his face with each breath.

He stopped in front of Fred, pointing toward the car. "Did you kids see who did this?"

All three of them shook their heads. "No, sir."

"Hmph!" The driver's eyes were filled with anger. "One of the neighbors called the police. Maybe they can find the troublemakers." He stormed back to the trolley and climbed in. A moment later, the door closed.

Alice pointed to the top of the trolley. "What is that boy doing?"

Fred looked where she pointed. "It looks like he's tying a rope to the cable that brings electricity from the wires to run the trolley."

"Why?" Steven asked.

Fred shook his head. "I don't know."

"Where did he come from?" Alice asked. "I didn't see him until a minute ago."

Fred shrugged. "Maybe he was lying down up there, hiding, while the driver was moving the car."

As the trolley started slowly, the boy jumped off, landing in a crouch on the street. Fred could see him clearly in the street lamp's light. He looked about fifteen. He was wearing a

35

black winter jacket and a tweed, billed hat.

The boy jumped up and started to run. As he raced past them, he grinned at Fred as though they shared a secret. Then he was gone, off around the building and down the alley.

Alice grabbed Fred's sleeve. "Look! The trolley is stopping!"

Sure enough, barely a block away, the trolley was rolling to a stop. Where the boy had jumped from the trolley, a black, thin shadow dangled from the electric wires above the street to the telegraph pole.

Fred snapped his fingers. "That's what that boy was doing on top of the trolley!"

"What?" Alice asked.

"What?" Steven repeated.

"He tied the rope to the telegraph pole. Then he climbed on top of the trolley and tied the other end to the cable that connects the trolley to the electric wires. When the trolley started off, the rope pulled the cable out of the trolley. Then the trolley couldn't get any electricity, so it stopped."

"I get it," Alice said.

"Everyone's getting off the trolley," Steven said.

By the light of a street lamp, they could see the driver climbing up the back of the trolley to see what was wrong. The passengers were lining up in the street, watching him.

Fred shook his head. "Boy, I bet the driver's going to be really mad now."

"Some of the passengers must have come from a costume party," Alice said. "See their fancy costumes? Dot was going to a fancy party with her parents tonight. She was bragging about the beautiful princess costume her mother was renting for her to wear."

Suddenly the passengers began throwing their arms in

36

front of their faces. Some raced for the trolley door to reboard.

"What's going on?" Fred said.

"What's happening?" Alice asked at the same time.

They started running toward the trolley. Fred's wooden sword banged against his leg. He kept a firm grip on the cloth bag that held his candy.

"Hey, wait up!" Alice called. She was having trouble running with her tin pail.

Fred stopped short. Alice almost tripped over him.

"It's eggs!" Fred cried.

Sure enough, now that they were closer, they could see a gang of older boys pummeling the trolley and its passengers with eggs. Yellow egg yolk blotched the sides of the trolley and ran down people's coats, costumes, hats, hair, and faces. The trolley driver was yelling at the boys. His yelling got louder when an egg landed right on his cap's shiny visor and dripped onto his nose. The boys were laughing and yelling while they hurled their white bombs.

"Good one!"

"Did ya see that shot? I should be a baseball pitcher!"

"Got a little egg on yer face?"

A siren cut through the night air. It came closer.

"We'd better get out of here," Fred said. "That must be the police. Remember the driver said someone had called them?"

"But we didn't do anything wrong," Alice argued.

"No," Fred agreed, "but we can't help the police. We'll just be in the way." *Besides, what if some of the older boys tried to say that Alice and Steven and I had tied the rope to the trolley? We couldn't prove we didn't. Uncle Donald and Aunt Lydia will be angry with me if I get their children in trouble.*

He turned to walk away. "Come on." He glanced back to

37

be sure Steven and Alice were following. They were, but Alice was already falling behind. She was watching the trolley over her shoulder. Impatience made him feel angry. "Hurry up, Alice."

Instead she stopped. Giggled.

"What's so funny?"

She pointed toward the passengers. "See the girl in the long blue dress with sequins, the one wearing the silver crown? That's Dot!"

Fred squinted, looking at the girl Alice pointed out. It was Dot. Smears of yellow blotted the blue dress.

While they watched, a small object hurled through the air and landed right in front of the crown. Dot screamed while egg yolk poured down her face. Then the older boys took off down the street.

Fred tugged at Alice's arm. "Let's go."

The sirens were growing louder as they turned the corner and started toward home.

CHAPTER 5

Alice's Birthday Party

"Did you hear that the police caught some of the boys who egged the trolley passengers?" Fred asked Alice two days later.

It was Saturday and Alice's ninth birthday. Fred had offered to help her get ready for her party that afternoon, so he came before the other guests arrived. He and Alice had just put the leaves in the dining room table to make it larger.

"Good. That was a nasty thing to do." Alice giggled. "But Dot did look funny with egg running down her face." She

39

pulled a tablecloth from a drawer in the dining room hutch. "Would you help me put this on the table?"

They each took an end of the long cloth and spread it over the dining room table. Fred could hear Aunt Lydia's voice coming from the kitchen, singing along to the music on the radio. "You're the cream in my coffee," she sang.

Fred and Alice grinned at each other across the table. It was a popular song, but Fred and Alice thought it a funny one.

Alice took china plates from the hutch and began setting them on the table. They had pink roses and were trimmed in silver. "Mother said I can use these for my party. Aren't they pretty?"

Fred nodded. He didn't see why women and girls cared what the plates you ate off of looked like, but he didn't see any point in arguing about it. "Why are you friends with Dot if you don't like her?"

Alice shrugged. "She can be fun sometimes, but when she's acting stuck up, I don't like her. Ever since her father started working for the Foshay Company, she thinks she's better than other kids. She's usually nice to me, but she's mean to some kids."

"Why?"

"She doesn't like to be friends with girls if she thinks they don't have enough money to buy nice clothes and things like that."

"That sounds dumb," Fred said.

Alice placed a little basket of paper and lace at each plate. "I made these. I'm going to fill them with nuts and let each guest take one home."

"Good idea. It must have taken you a while to make all of them."

Aunt Lydia came bustling into the room, humming another tune with the radio. A white apron with ruffles at the shoulders covered her dress. She was carrying a crystal platter. On it was a birthday cake with white frosting and pink roses. She set the platter down in the middle of the table. "What do you think?"

Alice leaned against the table and gave a gasp of delight. "Oh, Mother, it's beautiful!"

Aunt Lydia's blue eyes sparkled with pleasure.

"Isn't it pretty, Fred?" Alice asked, still staring at the cake.

Fred laughed. "Sure is, but who cares? It looks good enough to eat, and that's all that matters with a cake."

Aunt Lydia laughed with him, but Alice shook her head and looked at him as though he had no more brains than a toad.

Fred noticed the radio program change from music to the news.

"Mother, does Isabel have to be at the party?" Alice asked.

"She likes to play games and eat cake and ice cream just like you and your friends do," her mother reminded her.

"She gets in the way. She's only four—too young to play most of the games we like."

Aunt Lydia sighed. "Let her play some of the games. If she becomes bothersome, I'll take her in the kitchen and find something she can play by herself."

"Thanks, Mother."

Fred frowned. "Isn't the reporter talking about the Foshay Tower? Did something happen to it?"

They all quit talking and went to stand beside the radio.

"Mr. Foshay is bankrupt," the announcer said in crisp tones. "Two months ago he was hailed by some of the most powerful men in the world as one of them. A man of vision. Thirteen years ago he began with nothing to build an empire. Today he

41

is again reduced to nothing. Even the famous Foshay Tower, which bears his name, will be sold to pay his companies' bills. The receivers for the companies will be cutting costs to try to save them. Already a number of Foshay's employees have been fired in an attempt to save money."

The announcer told a little more about Mr. Foshay and his companies, but Fred didn't understand much of what he said. When the man went on to other news, Fred turned to Aunt Lydia. "What does bankrupt mean?"

"It means Mr. Foshay is broke, that his companies aren't making enough money to pay their bills."

Alice crossed her arms across her chest. "How could a man with as much money as Mr. Foshay has go broke? He has companies all over the United States and even in different countries."

"I heard him say something about stock," Fred said. "Did Mr. Foshay go broke because of the stock market crash last week?"

"Maybe," Aunt Lydia said. "The reporter said the companies didn't make enough money in sales to pay their bills. The money Mr. Foshay spent came from selling stock in the companies. With the stock market crash, people stopped buying stock. Maybe that's why he went broke." Her forehead puckered into a frown. "I didn't think it could happen so fast, though."

Alice looked worried. "Do you think Dot's father was one of the people who was fired?"

Her mother slipped an arm over Alice's shoulders. "I don't know. It might be best, though, if you didn't ask her about it today. Wait for her to bring it up. If her father did lose his job, Dot and her family are probably upset."

Alice and Fred nodded.

Aunt Lydia snapped off the radio and smiled brightly.

"Now I think it's time for you to change into your party dress, Alice. Your guests will be here soon. And you, Fred, may help me clean up the extra frosting while we wait for Alice."

Alice's new dress felt like it floated about her as she hurried down the stairs after she'd changed. The dress made her feel special and pretty. She liked the soft feel of the dark green velvet. A large white collar trimmed with lace circled the top of the dress. A green satin ribbon tied in a bow at the neck, its ties dangling almost to the dress's hem.

Soon the doorbell started ringing as Alice's guests arrived. Alice or her mother answered the door. Alice thanked each guest for the gaily wrapped gifts they brought. Fred piled the unopened gifts on a table in the living room. Steven hung up the guests' coats.

Dot was the last one to arrive. She thrust a small square gift tied with a golden ribbon toward Alice. "Here. Happy birthday."

Alice took the gift, blinking in surprise. "Thank you."

Dot doesn't sound like she's happy, Alice thought. Dot wasn't smiling. *I wonder if her father lost his job.* She wanted to ask Dot but remembered her mother's words and decided not to.

When Alice and Dot joined the others in the living room, the guests were talking about Halloween. There was lots of laughter as they shared funny stories about the night and described their costumes.

"Alice told me you went to a costume party, Dot," Fred said. "Did you have a good time?"

Alice darted him a sharp look. *How can he ask that without laughing?* she wondered. No one would ever know from his face or voice that he'd seen the egg attack.

43

Dot smiled for the first time that afternoon. She sat up straighter. "I had a wonderful time. It was a simply marvelous party. A band played and people danced." She smoothed the red curl that was shaped perfectly, as always, against her cheek. "I was dressed as a princess. My costume was rented, and it was beautiful, of course."

"I'm sure it was," Alice said, trying not to laugh. *Dot didn't say anything about the eggs!*

Alice glanced at Fred. He was pressing his lips together hard, but his eyes were filled with laughter.

Alice noticed her mother giving her and Fred a strange look. Dot may not have noticed something was strange with Fred's question, but Mother had!

"Oof!" Alice staggered a little as Isabel threw her arms about Alice's knees.

"Aren't we going to play games?" Isabel asked.

Alice pried Isabel's fingers loose. "Sure. How about pin the tail on the donkey?" That was a game even little Isabel could play.

"I'll get the donkey!" Isabel raced into the kitchen and came back clutching a gray stuffed donkey that Alice's mother had made just for the party.

Dot lost her smile when the game began and she was no longer the center of attention.

Alice was glad when quiet Inez won. She gave her a lace-edged handkerchief that she and her mother had chosen for gifts for the winners of the games. In case Fred or Steven won, they had also bought marbles.

The girls had seemed to enjoy watching little Isabel play, almost as much as they'd enjoyed playing the game themselves. When Alice suggested a game of forfeits, Inez said,

"Oh, that's too hard for Isabel. Let's play something else."

The other guests were quick to agree, even gloomy Dot. They played drop the handkerchief until everyone had had the handkerchief dropped behind them at least once.

When the game was over, Mother held out her hand to Isabel. "Will you come help me in the kitchen? We need to get things ready for the cake and ice cream."

Isabel went willingly. Mother winked at Alice on her way out of the room.

After a game of hide-the-thimble, Fred and Steven went to help Alice's mother make the ice cream. While they did that, Alice and her guests played forfeits. Then Mother called the guests to the dining room for their lunch. Alice was pleased when everyone said how pretty her cake was.

"What cute baskets," Inez said after everyone had sung "Happy Birthday" and Alice had blown out her candles.

"Thanks. I made them."

"Real ones would be better, of course," Dot said, fingering the lace on her basket handle. "I saw pretty little ones with red roses painted on them at Dayton's. They would make lovely favors."

Pain and anger swelled up inside Alice. After all the hours she'd spent making her baskets, Dot ruined them for her with her unkind remark.

"I'm sure the china baskets you saw are lovely," Inez said in her quiet voice. She ran a fingertip along the lace that edged her basket handle. "But they probably didn't have lace, and I like the lace. It's so pretty."

Alice saw Dot shake her head as if she thought it too bad Inez didn't know that china baskets were better than home-made ones.

45

"I don't care much about the lace." Fred made a face. "But at least Alice's baskets won't break if I drop them, and a china basket would break."

Alice smiled at her friends. A warm feeling filled her chest at their kind words.

A minute later, Mother entered with the pail of ice cream and a large scoop. She cut the cake and put the pieces on the pretty china, while Alice scooped the ice cream.

"Wa-a-a-aw!

Alice groaned. Why did one-year-old Frank have to choose now to start crying, when she and Mother were both busy? She glanced at Mother and held her breath. Would Mother ask her to take care of Frank?

"Wa-a-aw!"

Mother stopped cutting the cake, looked at Alice, and bit her bottom lip. Then she turned to Steven. "Will you check on your brother for me?"

Alice let out the breath she'd been holding and stuck her large spoon back in the pail of ice cream.

"I'll check on him," Dot said.

Alice looked up in surprise. Dot was sliding off her chair.

"Is he in the kitchen?" Dot asked.

"Yes." Mother smiled at her. "Thank you."

Dot smiled back at her. "I like babies." She hurried into the kitchen.

By the time the cake and ice cream had been served to everyone, the crying had stopped. Alice would have forgotten all about Frank if hadn't been for Dot's empty chair. She hadn't thought Dot would help out with Frank that way. *She isn't always so bad.*

Dot was the last of the guests to leave, even after Fred.

Alice handed Dot her coat, noticing it was made of chinchilla, the kind that was so popular that fall. When Dot was buttoning her coat, Alice thanked her for helping with Frank.

Dot shrugged. "He's kind of cute. I wish I had a little brother."

"Little brothers can be a pain sometimes."

"I suppose." Dot pulled on her mittens. She slipped the handle of her paper basket favor over a thumb.

"Thanks for coming to my party and for the present."

"You're welcome. It was a nice party, but it would have been more fun if you hadn't asked Inez. I don't understand why you like to have her around. None of the rest of our group likes her."

Alice's face felt hot with anger. She wanted to tell Dot how mean she thought she was, but she bit the words back. It was her party, and she was supposed to be nice to her guests.

"There's my Father. I'd better go. 'Bye!" Dot hurried out the door and down the sidewalk to where her father waited in a shiny new car.

Alice pushed the door shut as hard as she could. "Goodbye and good riddance," she grumbled, storming down the hall to the kitchen.

Mother looked up in surprise from the kitchen sink when Alice stomped into the room. "What's wrong? Didn't you like your party?"

Alice crossed her arms and dropped into a chair. "That Dot makes me so mad! I wish I'd never invited her to the party!"

"I thought she seemed nice. Frank likes her."

"A lot Frank knows."

Frank, who was playing on the floor with a kettle and wooden spoon, heard his name. He looked up at her and grinned.

Alice felt the warm spot around her heart she always felt when little Frank smiled at her. She bent forward and wrinkled her nose at him. "Anyone would like you, wouldn't they, little bug?"

"What did Dot do that made you so angry?" Mother asked.

Alice told her what Dot said about the baskets she'd made and about Inez.

Mother's usually smiling blue eyes grew serious as she listened. She wiped her hands on a towel and walked slowly across the room to sit down on a chair beside Alice.

"What did you say to Dot when she said these things?" Mother asked.

Alice folded her arms tightly over her chest again. "I didn't say anything. I remembered she was my guest and I was supposed to be nice to her. That's what Jesus says, too, isn't it? To be nice to people, to treat them the way we would want them to treat us."

"Yes, that's what Jesus said." Mother spoke slowly. "But I don't think Jesus meant that we should let other people say or do bad things."

"You mean, I didn't have to be nice back to her?" Alice was so surprised that some of her anger slipped away.

"Well, I don't think you should have been unkind to her. But maybe you could have told her that you like Inez, and you don't want to hear her saying unkind things about your other friends."

Alice thought for a minute. "You don't think that's being unkind to her?"

"I think it is being kind to other friends when you stand up for them."

Alice leaned against the wooden chair back. "I guess it is."

48

She wasn't sure she had the courage to stand up to Dot, though. All the other girls looked up to Dot. She might make everyone mad at her if she told Dot what she thought.

"Maybe," Mother said, "Dot was being ornery today because things aren't pleasant at home for her. Remember, her father may lose his job."

"I forgot. Do you think I should pray for Dot and her family?"

Mother smiled. "Prayer always helps."

CHAPTER 6
The Family Celebrates

Seated at the dining room table at Fred's house, Alice spread a napkin over her green velvet dress. She didn't want any Thanksgiving turkey or gravy to spill on her best outfit.

The Allertons had invited the Moes and the Harringtons to spend the holiday with them. It made sense, since they had the largest house.

The middle of the table was so covered with serving dishes that Alice could barely see Aunt Frances's pretty lace tablecloth. Alice's mouth watered at the wonderful smells of roast turkey and pumpkin pies.

"The pies are made from the pumpkins Steven and I grew," she told Addy, who was seated next to her. "We had to help Mother cut the pumpkin meat from the pumpkins. That was hard work."

Sixteen-year-old Addy smiled at her. "It will be worth all the hard work when you eat the pie today."

Alice nodded.

The men clapped and cheered when Fred and Alice's mothers carried in the turkey. It was golden brown and filled the huge silver platter.

Fred and Alice and Addy and the other children cheered when Aunt Frances tied an apron on Uncle Richard and told him to carve the turkey. Fred's father looked funny with the ruffled apron over his white shirt and tie.

"Did you hear about Amelia Earhart?" Fred asked as the food was passed around the table.

"Did something happen to her?" Alice asked. "Did her plane crash?"

Fred shook his head. "No. She set a new speed record for women pilots this week. One hundred and ninety-seven miles an hour!"

"Not too shabby for a lady," Uncle Erik said.

"Or for a man," Addy teased her father.

"What was the old record?" Uncle Erik asked.

"One hundred and fifty-four miles an hour," Fred answered promptly. "Amelia Earhart flew more than forty miles an hour faster! That's quite a jump."

"That woman seems determined to set one record after another," Uncle Erik said. "Last year she was the first woman to fly over the Atlantic Ocean."

Alice wondered if she would ever do anything the whole

51

world would talk about, important things like Amelia Earhart did. *I don't know what it would be. I don't want to fly airplanes!*

By the time the pumpkin pies were served, the men were talking about the stock market crash. It seemed to Alice the men had talked about Black Tuesday every time they'd been together for the last month. She was getting tired of all the talk of it.

Her father's dark eyes looked troubled. "I'm worried the crash will cause people all over the country to lose their jobs," he told Uncle Richard and Uncle Erik.

Alice's father was an engineer. He designed mill equipment. She looked at his worried face. *Does Father think he might lose his job?* The question made her stomach feel funny.

Uncle Richard leaned back in his chair and crossed his arms. "I think you're mistaken. Mostly the wealthy people who invest in stocks will lose money."

"I agree," Uncle Erik said.

Father shook his head. "I don't know. The twenties have been good years for most people but not for farmers. Now grain and livestock prices have followed the stock market. They're going lower and lower. The farmers aren't making much money on their products. And the flour mills like the one where I work depend on the farmers and their grain."

Uncle Erik smiled. "Farmers aren't going to quit growing grain. I think that's the least of the country's worries."

Alice could see her father wasn't as sure of that as Uncle Erik.

"When the stock market crashed, we didn't think it would affect many people in Minneapolis, either, did we?" Father asked. "But it did. Only a couple days later Mr. Foshay's companies went bankrupt. Thousands of his employees lost their jobs. The same thing could happen with other companies."

"President Hoover and powerful business leaders are trying to keep that from happening," Uncle Richard reminded him. "Already Hoover has met with top leaders from banking, industry, farms, and railroads. Business leaders have agreed not to lay men off or lower wages."

"That's right," Uncle Erik agreed. "Why, Henry Ford says he is raising wages at his automobile plants, just to prove he isn't afraid the country is in any trouble."

"And Hoover already has started a program to help farmers," Uncle Richard added. "Even the state government has agreed to spend more money on highway jobs."

"I interviewed some of the top banking and business leaders in Minneapolis for the newspaper," Uncle Erik told Alice's father. "They say business has never been better. Manufacturers here even sent a wire to President Hoover. They promised him they wouldn't fire people to save their companies money."

Alice's father shook his head. "I hope things are as good here as the people told you, but I'm not so sure."

Isabel leaned against Alice's legs. "Will you play dolls with me?"

"Sure." Alice was tired of hearing the men talk about money and business troubles, anyway.

Isabel reached for Addy's hand. "You play, too."

"Okay. Sounds like fun." She smiled down at Isabel. "But maybe Alice and I should help the women with the dishes first."

"Go on and play," Fred's mother said. "You'll be helping us more by keeping her out from under foot."

So the girls went in the living room, and Fred and Steven went outside to play.

Before long, the men came into the living room, too. They wanted to listen to the radio.

Her father's talk of the Foshay companies had reminded Alice of Dot. Her friend had never said whether her father lost his job when Mr. Foshay's companies went bankrupt. *Uncle Erik works for the newspaper,* she thought. *He knows lots that happens in the city. Maybe he knows.*

She got up from the floor, leaving her doll behind, and went to lean against his chair.

He smiled at her. "Having a good time?"

She nodded. "Uncle Erik, do you know who lost their jobs at Mr. Foshay's companies?"

He nodded. "Some of them. Why?"

"My friend's father worked for Mr. Foshay. He had an important job and a fancy office in the Foshay Tower."

"What is his name?"

"Mr. Lane. I think his first name is Albert."

Uncle Erik nodded. "I'm sorry. I'm afraid your friend's father did lose his job. From what I've heard, he hasn't found another job yet."

Alice took a deep breath, then let it out in a sigh. "I thought maybe he'd lost his job, but I didn't dare ask my friend."

Uncle Erik patted her hand. "I'm sure he'll find another job soon."

Alice nodded.

Uncle Richard turned on the radio, and Alice went back to playing dolls with Addy and Isabel.

"I heard what you and Uncle Erik were talking about," Addy said, buttoning a pink corduroy coat on Isabel's doll for the little girl. "Who is the friend you mentioned? Do I know her?"

Alice told her about Dot, reminding her that she'd seen her

on the observation deck at the Foshay Tower.

Alice always liked talking to Addy. Even though Addy was almost grown up, she didn't treat Alice like a little girl. Addy listened to her. When Alice asked her questions, she answered them seriously.

Now she told Addy how proud Dot had been of her father's job and how snobbish she'd acted at the birthday party.

"Maybe Dot acted so awful at the party because she was upset about her father losing his job," Addy said.

"That's what Mother said."

"You know, Alice, lots of times it's hard to be nice to people when we're hurting."

Alice helped Isabel diaper one of her dolls. While Alice and Addy talked, Isabel sang lullabies to her dolls.

"Sometimes Dot does nice things, like when she helped with Frank at my party," Alice told Addy, "but sometimes it's hard for me to like her. Is that awful of me?"

"I don't think so," Addy said slowly. "It sounds like you try to be nice to her, and that's what's important."

"Even if Dot is unhappy because her father lost his job, she should live by the Golden Rule and treat others the way she likes to be treated, don't you think?"

Addy nodded. "Absolutely."

Suddenly Addy started coughing again. She coughed and coughed for what seemed a long time to Alice.

Uncle Richard turned down the radio and came to kneel beside Addy when she stopped coughing. "This isn't the first time I've heard you cough today, young lady. Do you have another cold?"

Addy laughed weakly then started coughing again. When

she stopped, she said, "It's seems I've had this cold for months. It won't go away."

Uncle Richard put a finger under her chin and lifted her face so he could see it better in the light coming through the living room windows. "You look a bit tired." He frowned. "Lost some weight, too, since I saw you last, haven't you?"

"Maybe a little," she admitted.

"I want to see you in my office tomorrow for a checkup."

Addy shook her head. "It's only a cold."

"Tomorrow," Uncle Richard repeated, standing.

Uncle Erik, Addy's father, was leaning forward in his chair, watching and listening. "You don't think it's something serious, do you, Richard?" he asked.

Uncle Richard looked at him. "It's probably only a cold, but it won't hurt to check it out."

"But, Uncle Richard—" Addy protested.

"She'll be there," Uncle Erik said firmly.

Uncle Richard turned the radio back up. Music filled the room. The men started talking about business and money again.

Addy leaned close to whisper to Alice, "Parents always worry so!"

Isabel rested a hand against Addy's cheek. "Are you sick?"

Addy smiled and shook her head. "I have a cold, that's all."

A moment later, she began coughing again.

CHAPTER 7
The Bell Ringer

Monday morning, all the students at school were talking about the exciting news. Over the holiday, Commander Byrd had flown over the South Pole!

In class, Mrs. Sims called everyone up to the front of the room. They stood around her desk so they could all see when she showed them the globe of the world.

Mrs. Sims pointed to the very bottom of the globe, an area covered in white. "This is what the commander flew over. Everything is ice and snow there." Then she pointed to the very top of the globe. "This is the North Pole. Commander Byrd flew over that three years ago. He is the only man in the world who has flown over both the North and South Poles."

"Was it dangerous?" Alice asked.

Mrs. Sims nodded. "Very. It's a long way from almost every civilized place. If his plane had crashed, it would have been hard for anyone to rescue him and his pilot and navigator."

After lunch, the entire school was called to the auditorium. Mrs. Sims stopped Alice on the way into the large room. "I'd like you to help us with the program today. Would you do that?"

Alice was surprised, but she agreed. "Yes. What do you want me to do?"

"Come with me."

Alice followed tall, skinny Mrs. Sims down the side aisle and up onto the stage. At the edge of the stage, in front of the large maroon velvet curtains that hid the back of the stage from the audience, Mrs. Sims handed her a large brass bell with a wooden handle.

"When everyone is in their seats," Mrs. Sims told her, "someone in a costume will come running down the center aisle. When you see that person, start ringing your bell. There will be other students ringing bells, too. When the person in the costume gets up on stage, you can stop ringing the bell."

When Mrs. Sims left, Alice stayed where she was. She felt funny up on stage, even though she knew most of the other students couldn't see her very well. Where she stood it was dark. The lights were on the center of the stage.

She looked about the auditorium, trying to find the other bell ringers. There was another on the opposite end of the stage. Up in the balcony, ringers stood at each end. She squinted to see past the students who were still crowding into the auditorium. At the back of the downstairs area, a bell ringer was positioned at each corner.

Who is coming? Alice wondered. *What kind of costume will the person be wearing?*

58

Finally everyone was seated. The doors to the auditorium were closed. Alice waited for the principal or a teacher to come on stage to tell everyone to quiet down. But no one went on stage, and the students kept talking. The excited buzz of their voices was loud.

Then Alice saw one of the doors open. Someone in a green costume slipped inside. The person looked like one of Santa's elves. The costume included a hat with points. On the ends of the points were balls. Around the elf's neck was a wide collar with more points.

With a small gasp, Alice realized she was supposed to be ringing her bell. The bell was so big that she had to hold the wooden handle with both hands to ring it. She pressed her lips together hard and rang the bell as hard as she could.

The other bell ringers began ringing their bells right after Alice did. At the sound of the bells, the children stopped talking. Alice could see them turning in their seats, stretching their necks to see what all the ringing was about, and pointing to the bell ringers and the funny-looking elf.

The elf began running down the aisle, waving at the students with one hand and ringing a small bell with the other.

So that's what this meeting is all about! Alice thought. *It's a visit from the Bell Ringer for Christmas Seals!*

Alice had no idea who the Bell Ringer really was. The one-piece costume covered all of the person's body except for his or her face. All she could tell was that the Bell Ringer was short and slender.

The Bell Ringer ran up the steps to the stage waving at the students and ringing the bell all the way. In the middle of the stage, the Bell Ringer stopped.

"Hello, everyone!" the Bell Ringer called.

59

Alice knew from the sound of the voice that the Bell Ringer was a young woman.

The Bell Ringer lifted her bell high above her head and rang it. "Do you know who I am?"

The students yelled back, "The Bell Ringer!" Their voices echoed off the auditorium walls.

"That's right," the Bell Ringer called back. "Why am I here?"

"For Christmas Seals!" everyone screamed.

All the students knew the Bell Ringer. Every year the Bell Ringer came to school. And every year the Bell Ringer visited downtown with Santa.

"Right again," the Bell Ringer said. "I'm here to tell you how each and every one of you can be a soldier in a war. You won't have to carry guns to fight this war. This isn't a war to take lives; this is a war to save lives. We're declaring war on TB. That's tuberculosis. TB is a disease of the lungs. How many of you know someone who has TB or who died from TB?"

Hands went up all over the auditorium.

The Bell Ringer nodded her head. The balls bounced on the ends of the spikes on her costume hat. "That's what I thought. Lots of people have TB, don't they? Did you know that over the last two hundred years, TB has killed more people in the United States and Europe than any other disease?"

Students shook their heads.

"It's true," the Bell Ringer said. "Sometimes other diseases kill many people at one time. Eleven years ago there was a flu epidemic that killed more people at one time than any disease for hundreds of years. But most years, TB kills more people than any other disease. Most of the people who catch TB are young, between fifteen and thirty-five years old. Two-thirds of the people who catch TB die within five years."

Children stared at the Bell Ringer, wide-eyed. Some whispered to each other about the disease.

"The reason so many people die," the Bell Ringer told them, "is because doctors and scientists don't know what causes TB and don't have any drugs to cure it. Some of the treatments help, but we need a cure. Right?" The Bell Ringer leaned toward the auditorium with a hand behind her ear.

"Right!" the students agreed in a yell that bounced off the walls.

"Do you want to be soldiers in the war against TB?" The Bell Ringer leaned forward with her hand behind her ear again.

"Yes!" Alice yelled with the rest of the kids.

"Good!" The Bell Ringer rang her bell again.

Alice started ringing her bell, too. The Bell Ringer grinned at her. Then the other students with bells began ringing them. The students in the audience began cheering.

When the noise died down, the Bell Ringer called, "How do we fight the war on TB?"

"We sell Christmas Seals!" the students answered.

"That's right. We sell Christmas Seals." The Bell Ringer's voice dropped to a loud talk. "Christmas Seals are like stamps. They can be used to seal Christmas cards and other envelopes or for decorating Christmas packages and letters or for anything else you can think of. The important thing is to raise money to fight TB by selling them. Right?"

"Right!"

"The money raised by Christmas Seals goes to research to find the cause and a cure for TB. The students who sell the most Christmas Seals will have their choice of prizes. But the real prize is that which each of us will earn by giving hope to people with a terrible disease."

The Bell Ringer told them that the following weekend, all the church bells and courthouse chimes and firehouse gongs would ring to remind people to buy Christmas Seals.

When the students left the auditorium, Dot and some of Alice's other friends waited for her. They all wanted to know how she ended up being a bell ringer. After she told them, one of the girls told of an uncle who had TB.

"It was awful," she told them. "He lost lots of weight and was real skinny. He coughed all the time. Sometimes he even coughed up blood."

"Blood!" Alice cringed.

Her friend nodded. "He had to go away to a sanatorium, where people with TB stay. That was a couple years ago. I haven't seen him since."

Inez said, "I hear that the doctors send people with TB to sanatoriums to die."

Alice shuddered. "Sanatoriums must be awful places." In her imagination, she saw a big building with lots of tombstones around it.

"Sometimes the doctors take out the patient's ribs," Dot told them in a voice that sounded like she was telling ghost stories.

"Can they do that?" Alice felt her own ribs. They were bones that made her chest feel hard.

Dot shrugged. "They do. Then the patient looks strange for the rest of his life. Like he's crippled."

Alice was glad when they reached their classroom and couldn't talk about TB anymore. It was scary to think about. The stories the girls told made her feel creepy.

That evening, Alice heard a knock on the door. When she

answered it, she was surprised to find Fred's parents at the door.

"I didn't know you were coming over tonight." She held the door open wide, smiling. She liked Uncle Richard and Aunt Frances.

The adults smiled back, but their smiles were smaller than usual.

"We came to see your parents," Aunt Frances told her. Alice hung their winter coats in the hall closet, then led her aunt and uncle into the living room. Mother looked up from her mending and Father from his newspaper to greet them.

"What a lovely surprise!" Mother said, setting aside the shirt she was mending.

Uncle Richard and Aunt Frances sat down. Alice dropped to the floor beside Steven, where the two of them had been playing jacks before Alice answered the door. Alice bounced the small rubber ball, scooped up some many-sided metal jacks, and caught the ball in the same hand. She bounced the ball again.

"I'm afraid you won't think this is a lovely visit when you hear our news," Aunt Frances said.

Alice forgot to catch the ball. She glanced over her shoulder at Aunt Frances.

Her parents leaned forward in their chairs. "What's wrong?" Father asked.

"Remember I told Addy to come to my office for a check-up last week?" Uncle Richard asked.

"Yes, for her cold," Father said.

"It wasn't a cold," Uncle Richard told him. "The test results came back today. Addy has TB."

CHAPTER 8
The TB Test

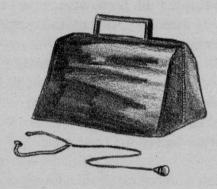

Alice felt like she'd been frozen in a sheet of ice. She couldn't move. Her chest hurt so bad she could hardly breathe. TB! Sweet, pretty Addy had that awful disease!

"TB!" she heard her mother whisper.

"Have you told Addy and her parents?" Father asked.

"Yes," Uncle Richard said.

"Addy is Erik and Esther's only child. This must be so frightening for them," Mother said in a soft voice. "Poor Addy."

Alice remembered her friends' stories about TB. Pictures filled her mind of people without ribs, coughing up blood and living in houses where everyone died.

She dropped her ball and jacks and hurried over to her mother. "She *doesn't* have TB! She doesn't! It's only a cold. She told me so. Addy said it's only a cold!"

Mother put her arms about Alice and pulled her close. Alice held her tight. Her throat started to hurt, her eyes grew hot, and she started to cry.

"I don't want Addy to have TB," she whispered through her tears.

"We wish she didn't have it, too," Mother said, "but she does. We can't help her by pretending it isn't true. The best things we can do for her right now are to love her and pray for her. Uncle Richard is going to see that Addy gets the best medical attention possible, isn't that right, Richard?"

Alice sniffled, wiped at her tears with the back of her hand, and looked at Uncle Richard.

His dark eyes looked gravely into hers. "That's right. I'll do everything I can for her."

Alice thought his words should make her feel better, but they didn't help very much. She still ached inside for Addy.

Uncle Richard shifted his attention to her parents. "TB is very easy to catch. Your family will have to be tested to see whether any of you have caught it from Addy. So will our family, of course, and Erik and Esther."

"When?" Father asked.

"Come to my office tomorrow, and I'll test all of you."

While Father and Mother saw Uncle Richard and Aunt Frances to the door, Alice sat in Mother's chair, her knees drawn up under her chin. She knew Steven sat in the middle of the living room floor surrounded by their jacks, staring at her, but she ignored him.

"TB is very easy to catch." That's what Uncle Richard had

said. Other people in their family might have TB, too. *Maybe even me,* Alice thought.

Fear curled through her.

When Alice opened her eyes the next morning, Mother was sitting on the bed with her hands on Alice's shoulder.

"It's all right," Mother was saying. "Everything is all right. It was only a bad dream."

"A dream," Alice repeated. She remembered now. In the dream, she'd been walking among the tombstones that surrounded a big house. Then a big black creature started chasing her. She ran as fast as she could, but the tombstones kept getting in her way and slowing her down. She'd screamed and screamed for help, but no one had come.

But it was only a dream, she reminded herself. "How did you know I was having a bad dream?"

"You were screaming," Mother told her, "so I came and woke you."

"When do we go to Uncle Richard's office for the TB test?"

"After school. We'll all go to Uncle Richard's office together."

It was a long day at school. Alice didn't tell any of her friends about Addy or the tests she and her family would have to take. It was too scary. She didn't want to talk about it yet.

In the waiting room at Uncle Richard's office that afternoon, Alice looked around. Aunt Frances and Fred were there, and Uncle Erik and Aunt Esther, but not Addy.

"Where's Addy?" Alice asked Aunt Esther. "Didn't she come?"

"No, she's at home in bed."

"Oh." Alice didn't know what to say. Her question had been silly, she realized. Addy didn't need a test to see whether she'd caught TB. Addy already knew she had it.

Aunt Esther's eyes looked red and swollen, like she'd been crying. The sight of them made Alice uncomfortable. She didn't know what to say to make Aunt Esther feel better.

Mother took Aunt Esther's hands in hers. "We've been thinking about you. Are you doing okay?"

Aunt Esther nodded and took a shaky breath. "I think so. It's all such a shock."

"I'd like to visit Addy, if that's all right," Mother said.

"Richard says she mustn't see anyone but her father and me for now," Aunt Esther told her. "Addy needs to lie flat on her back and rest her lungs and stay away from any excitement, Richard says."

"She has to do as the doctor orders, of course," Mother said with a small smile. "Tell her we are all thinking of her and praying for her."

Aunt Esther nodded.

Being close to Aunt Esther made Alice uncomfortable. She could almost feel her aunt hurting, but she couldn't help her.

Alice slid onto a chair beside Fred. Steven and Isabel looked at books at a little table Uncle Richard kept in the corner just for kids. Alice watched them, but she wasn't thinking about them.

Fred was quieter than usual. He wasn't looking at any magazines or books, either.

Alice reached out and touched the back of one of his hands. "Are you scared?" She asked the question in a low voice, so no one else could hear.

He didn't answer right away, just stared at the floor and bit his bottom lip. "A little," he said finally.

"Me, too."

He squeezed her hand.

"I wish Addy weren't sick," he admitted.

"Me, too."

Fred's hands balled into fists. "I'm going to sell more Christmas Seals than anyone in Minneapolis. Maybe if we raise enough money, somebody will find a medicine that will cure Addy."

"I hope so," Alice whispered.

A few minutes later Alice and her family went into Uncle Richard's office. Her uncle smiled at her. "Do you want to go first, Alice? You can show your brothers and sister how to do it and that there's nothing to be frightened of."

She didn't want to go first. She didn't want to have the test at all. But she knew she had to have it done, so she just nodded.

Uncle Richard rolled up her sleeve and smiled at her again. "This won't hurt."

Alice couldn't say anything. Fear made her throat feel like a big rubber ball was stuck in it. Her heart raced as she watched Uncle Richard scratch a small area on her arm with a needle. "See, I was right," he said, still smiling. "It didn't hurt, did it?"

She shook her head.

Gently, he taped a square of gauze over the area he'd scratched with the needle.

Alice swallowed the lump in her throat. "Do I. . .do I—" She could hardly get the words out. She tried again. "Do I have TB?"

Uncle Richard's face grew sober. "We can't tell right away.

In a few days, we'll take the gauze off your arm and check the area I scratched today. Then we'll know."

She pressed her lips together hard.

Uncle Richard laid his hand against her cheek. "Don't be too frightened, Alice. Most people who are exposed to TB don't get the disease."

Alice tried to smile at him, but she could tell it was only a little wobbly smile.

Every night, Alice's nightmare returned. The big black creature never caught her, but it chased her in her dreams night after night. After the first couple nights, she didn't want to go to sleep, but she had to.

She was glad for the morning sunshine and glad to go to school where she had something other than Addy and TB to think and talk about.

Later that week Mrs. Sims assigned parts for the Christmas play the students would put on later that month. Alice was to be one of the stars.

Only a little star, Alice thought. She would have liked to have a bigger part, but only one girl could be Mary. All the other big parts were for boys, she remembered: shepherds and wise men and Joseph.

Alice smiled at Inez when Mrs. Sims told Inez that she would play Mary. *Inez will make a nice Mary,* Alice thought.

"But I want to be Mary," Dot complained.

Mrs. Sims smiled brightly at her. "You're to be one of the stars, Dot."

Dot stamped her foot. "I don't *want* to be a star. I want to be Mary!"

Alice stared at her in surprise. Even though she wanted to

play the part of Mary, too, she would never behave like Dot was.

"Dot can be Mary if she wants," Inez said quietly. "I don't mind being a star."

"You will make a wonderful Mary," Mrs. Sims said firmly. "And Dot will do nicely among the stars."

Dot crossed her arms and sulked while Mrs. Sims finished assigning parts.

Alice glanced at Dot's face. Usually she thought Dot was pretty, but with the sulk on her face, Dot didn't look pretty at all. Alice was glad she hadn't put on a scene like Dot over what her part would be in the program.

When Mrs. Sims read the play through for them and explained the parts, Alice discovered that this year her part sounded like fun. She and a number of other girls weren't going to *be* stars. Instead they would *carry* stars. The star carriers would wear blue dresses with silver sashes. They'd carry silver stars on sticks.

"After all," Mrs. Sims told them, "although we hear of one extra-bright star that led the wise men, there were other stars that made the night sky beautiful. We want to have lots of pretty stars dancing in the sky in our program when the angels tell the shepherds Jesus has come."

That very afternoon, the class began getting ready for the Christmas program. The star carriers were put to work cutting stars six inches wide out of poster board. Then they put glue on the stars and sprinkled them with silver glitter.

Dot and Alice worked side by side. Dot was still pouting. "I should play Mary," she told Alice in a voice low enough that Mrs. Sims couldn't hear her. "Inez is too plain to play Mary."

"I think Inez is pretty," Alice told her. "She's nice, too."

Dot just sniffed. "She's too shy to play the part."

"There's nothing wrong with being shy," Alice said.

Lately it seemed to Alice that Dot had been grumpy a lot. Alice tried to remember what her mother and Addy had said about Dot being unhappy because her father had lost his job at the Foshay Tower, but it wasn't always easy to be nice to her. Besides, he had lost his job over a month ago. That was a long time ago. Maybe he had a new one by now.

Alice dipped her small wooden spreader into the jar of white glue and spread the glue on her star. She glanced at Dot out of the corner of her eye. Dot still had never said anything about her father losing his job. Maybe she would be nicer if someone told her they were sorry about it.

She took a deep breath. So no one else would hear, she spoke softly. "I'm sorry your father lost his job, Dot."

Dot looked at her, her green eyes wide with surprise. She didn't say anything, just stared at her with her wooden glue stick in one hand.

Alice tried again. "Has he found another job yet?"

"No." Dot went back to work.

"I'm sorry."

"You don't have to be sorry for me." Dot's voice was low but filled with anger. "Father has plenty of money."

Alice didn't know what to say, so she went back to work.

"Did you sell many Christmas Seals yet?" Dot asked.

Alice knew then that Dot didn't want to talk about her father. "No." The Christmas Seals made her think of Addy again. "My cousin has TB. We just found out a couple days ago."

Dot whirled to stare at her. "She must live in an awful place. Only filthy people get TB."

Anger swirled through Alice. "That's not true!"

"Is so!"

71

"Is not! You take that back, Dot Lane!"

"I won't! It *is* true!"

"Oh, you. . .you. . . !" Alice couldn't think of anything mean enough to call Dot.

Dot pushed at Alice's shoulder.

Alice pushed back.

Dot looked down at the place Alice had shoved her. "My dress! Look what you've done to my dress!"

Alice's stomach turned a somersault. The glue from the wooden spreader had come off in a white glob on Dot's red plaid jumper.

Before she could apologize, Mrs. Sims was standing between them, fists on her bony hips. "What are you two arguing about?"

"Look what she did to my dress!" Dot pointed at the glue spot.

Mrs. Sims shook her head. "Alice Harrington, I would never have thought you would do such a thing."

"But Dot started it. She pushed me!"

"I don't want to hear about it." Mrs. Sims held up both her hands. "Neither of you behaved properly. I heard you yelling at each other. You will both stay after school and write one hundred times, 'I will not yell in the classroom.' "

"But—"

"No buts from either of you," Mrs. Sims demanded. "Finish your stars, and no more arguments."

They did as they were told, but anger burned in Alice's chest the whole time they worked on the stars.

Her feet dragged on the way home, in spite of the crisp December weather and the snowflakes coming down on a brisk breeze. Her parents were sure to ask why she was so late coming home. They'd be angry when she told them about the argument and that she'd gotten glue on Dot's dress. But Dot shouldn't have said that awful thing about Addy.

When she turned the corner onto her street, she was surprised to see Uncle Richard's car in front of her house. She hurried the rest of the way. Once inside, she dropped her books on the hall table and snapped open her boots. She was pulling off her coat when she walked into the living room.

Mother looked across the room and smiled at her. "There you are! What took you so long getting home?"

Alice opened her mouth to answer, but before she could, Mother said, "Uncle Richard has come to look at our arms. He's checked the rest of us. You're the last one."

Alice's stomach felt like something was jumping around in it. She'd been so upset about Dot that she'd forgotten for a little while that she might have TB, too.

Uncle Richard held out a hand toward her and smiled. "Why don't you come over here and let me take that gauze off?"

Alice walked slowly across the room to the overstuffed chair where he sat and held out her arm. Alice held her breath while he pushed up the sleeve of her school dress and gently began to remove the gauze and tape.

CHAPTER 9
Saying Good-bye

Alice could feel her heart beating like it was a drum, fast and hard and loud. *What will Uncle Richard see? Do I have TB?*

She didn't dare ask the questions out loud. She was afraid of the answers.

Uncle Richard peeled the gauze and tape back slowly, holding her arm beneath the light from the floor lamp. He peered at her arm.

Alice's heart beat faster.

Then he grinned up at her. "It looks just the way we want it to look. No TB."

Alice felt like something heavy had rolled off her shoulders. She grinned back at him.

"Thank You, God," she heard Mother whisper.

Yes, thank You, God, Alice prayed silently.

She looked at her parents. They were both smiling. Suddenly Alice remembered that Uncle Richard had already looked at the rest of her family's arms. She hadn't even asked what he'd seen! She was ashamed she'd thought only of herself.

"Did. . .did anyone. . .is everyone. . . ?" She didn't know how to put her question into words.

"We are all fine." Mother smiled at her.

Alice smiled back. "Good." She rolled down her sleeve and looked back at Uncle Richard. "What about you and Aunt Frances and Fred and Uncle Erik and Aunt Esther?"

Uncle Richard leaned back in his chair. "We're all fine. I'm sure many of us caught the germs, but they didn't develop into TB. Most people who are exposed to the disease don't become ill from it. Those who do become ill usually become very ill."

"Like Addy."

"Yes." He nodded. "Like Addy."

"What kind of treatment will you be giving her?" Mother asked Uncle Richard.

"Well, I've put her on a diet with lots of milk and eggs. That's thought to be good for TB patients. She needs to keep as still as possible and rest her lungs in a place where there is plenty of fresh air. I've arranged for her to enter a sanatorium right after Christmas."

A sanatorium! The happiness Alice had felt upon finding she and her family did not have TB fled. In its place, horror washed through her. Uncle Richard was sending Addy to one of those awful places where people were sent to die!

"Have you sold many Christmas Seals?" Fred asked Alice one morning the next week. They were standing in the school hallway before classes started.

Alice shook her head. "Some, but not a lot." Actually, she'd only sold them to her parents. She hadn't even tried to sell to anyone else.

"I've sold quite a few. I go out every afternoon after school and sell them."

"Where do you go?" Alice asked.

"To houses. Sometimes I go downtown and sell them on the street or in stores."

Alice stared at him, surprised. "You go all the way downtown to sell them?"

"Sure. It's a great place to sell them. There are lots of people down there doing their Christmas shopping."

"I hadn't thought of that."

"Would you like to go with me this afternoon?" he asked.

"I. . .I can't. I have to work on my outfit for the Christmas play." *It's not a real lie,* Alice told herself, trying to push away the guilty feeling filling her chest. *I do have to work on my outfit, but I could do it another time.*

"Oh. Maybe we can go together tomorrow."

"Maybe. I'd better go to class now."

Fred's eyebrows scrunched together as he gave her a strange look. "The bell won't ring for another five minutes."

"I want to ask Mrs. Sims something before class starts. See you later." She flashed him a smile and hurried toward her classroom.

Her guilt grew. She'd told another lie. She didn't need to be at the classroom early. But she didn't like talking about Christmas Seals. She wasn't going to sell any more, either, even with Fred. The Christmas Seals reminded her of Addy. *I don't want to think about Addy or TB. All it does is make me sad.*

Alice found excuses for not going with Fred to sell Christmas Seals until he quit asking her to join him. She didn't even want to go with their families when Fred received his prize for selling so many Christmas Seals.

Everyone in both families admired the clock Fred chose as his prize. He'd had his choice of a watch or clock or toy plane. "I didn't quite make my goal," he told Alice while her parents admired the clock. "I wanted to sell more Christmas Seals than anyone else in Minneapolis. Instead, I only tied for first."

"You did a great job." Uncle Richard placed a large hand on Fred's shoulder. "I'm proud of you and all the hard work you put into this."

The rest of the family told Fred they felt the same way.

Fred beamed. "I didn't care about the prize. I only wanted to help Addy."

Alice walked away. She wished people would stop talking about Addy. *If Uncle Richard is sending Addy to the sanatorium, it's too late to help her by selling Christmas Seals.* She rubbed her fingers hard over her tear-filled eyes.

Christmas Day, Alice woke up screaming. She'd had that bad dream again.

Mother smoothed Alice's hair. Her eyes looked troubled. "I'm beginning to worry about all these nightmares you're having, Alice."

Alice didn't like them, either!

Mother winked. "I bet I know what will make you forget those old nightmare monsters this morning. Let's get the rest of the family up and go see whether Santa's been here yet."

Alice sat up quick. "Okay!" As soon as Mother stood up, Alice threw back her quilt and slipped out of bed.

At the door, Mother turned around. "Would you like to wear your Christmas play costume when we go to the Moes later today? I'm sure Addy would like to see it, since she couldn't go to the play."

All the horror and sadness Alice felt for Addy came back. Even the thought of Christmas presents wouldn't make it go away. "All right."

That afternoon, the Allertons and Harringtons went together to visit Addy. Uncle Richard didn't want Addy out of bed, so everyone filed into her bedroom. They all wore gauze masks on their faces. Uncle Richard told them the masks would help keep the TB germs away from them.

Addy was sitting up in bed, pillows plumped behind her. A small Christmas tree with shiny red and blue balls stood on top of a chest of drawers.

"We've missed you, Addy," Alice's mother said. "How are you feeling?"

Addy's smile was wide. "I feel fine, except for my old cough."

"We've brought you some gifts," Steven said.

Alice stood with her back against the wall, as far away from Addy as she could get. She was quiet while the others oohed and aahed over the presents Addy opened.

Sometimes Addy would start coughing. Then everyone would be quiet until she could stop coughing and talk like normal again. Every time she coughed, Alice grew sadder.

Addy's parents had given her a radio so she would have something to listen to during long days of resting at the sanatorium. Fred's parents gave her a book of poetry. Alice's family gave her a box of pretty stationery and a pen. "So you have no excuse for not writing us letters," Alice's mother told her.

Fred's gift was the last one opened. He leaned against the end of the bed while Addy carefully removed the gift wrap. His eyes were shining with eagerness. *What had he given Addy?* Alice wondered.

Her mouth dropped open in surprise when Addy pulled Fred's gift from its box. Fred had given her his clock!

"What a beautiful clock." Addy smiled at Fred. "Thank you."

"It's the clock I won for selling Christmas Seals," he told her. "I thought you might take it with you to the sanatorium. Every time you look at it, you can remember how children all over the United States sell Christmas Seals so scientists and doctors can find a cure for TB."

Addy blinked hard. Alice thought she saw tears on her lashes. "I will take it with me, Fred. It will be a wonderful reminder of people's love on days I'm feeling lonely. It's the best gift ever."

"Let's sing Christmas carols," Alice's mother suggested.

"May I sing, too?" Addy asked Uncle Richard.

Alice glanced at Uncle Richard. She thought he looked sad. "No," he said. "I'm sorry, but it wouldn't be good to strain your lungs that way."

For a moment, Addy's lips turned down in a frown. Then she smiled. "Well, then, I'll just lay here and enjoy my Christmas carolers."

The families sang "Silent Night" and "The First Noël." Then Alice's mother said, "Since you weren't able to see the

Christmas program Alice's class put on, Addy, would you like Alice to show you the part she played?"

"That would be wonderful! I was so sorry I had to miss your program, Alice."

Mother helped Alice off with her coat.

"What a beautiful costume!" Addy said.

Her compliment made Alice feel warm inside. "The dress is blue like the sky," she told Addy, "and the silver ribbon around the top of the skirt is shiny like the stars."

"We'll sing the song for you," Mother said, "and you do the dance the stars did during the program."

"I wasn't the only star bearer," Alice told Addy. "It's better with everyone."

"I'll pretend they are all here," Addy said.

Mother started the song, and the others joined in:

> *"Love came down at Christmas,*
> *Love all lovely, love divine;*
> *Love was born at Christmas,*
> *Star and angels gave the sign."*

While they sang, Alice danced. She held the long wand with the sparkling silver star high above her and circled the room. Sometimes she twirled around. Other times she whirled the star fast, so it caught the sunlight and sparkled more than ever. She danced through all three verses of the song.

When she was done, everyone in the room clapped. Alice felt her cheeks grow warm, and her chest filled with happiness that they had liked her dance.

"That was beautiful," Addy said. "I wouldn't be at all surprised if the stars danced from happiness when Jesus was born."

Uncle Richard cleared his throat. "I hate to cut short everyone's good time, but we mustn't tire Addy out. We've already stayed longer than is probably good for her."

"I wish I could hug each of you good-bye," Addy said, "but I wouldn't want you to catch TB from me. I'm so glad all of you came to see me for Christmas."

Each person told Addy good-bye. When it was Alice's turn, Addy said, "Thank you for dancing for me. I'll miss seeing you while I'm at the sanatorium."

"I'll miss you, too." Alice's throat hurt when she said the words. Her eyes heated with tears until Addy was only a blur. The tears rolled down her cheeks as she left Addy's room. They didn't stop falling all the way home.

Will I ever see Addy again? Alice wondered, wiping at her tears. *Why can't Addy stay at home with her family instead of being sent away to die in a sanatorium?*

CHAPTER 10

News from Addy

"Ugh!" Alice grunted and shifted her load. The braided rug she carried was large and heavy. She couldn't see over or around it while she carried it down the back steps into the yard. She felt for the bottom step with the sole of her shoe and stepped carefully onto the sidewalk.

"Let me help you with that." Mother took one end of the rolled rug. "There's room for it on the farthest clothesline."

Together they carried the rug over and heaved it across the line.

Alice was panting slightly when she got back to the sidewalk. She turned and looked at the clothesline. Rugs of different colors and sizes made bright squares and circles of color against the May green of new leaves and grass.

Mother shooed away a blackbird who had stopped to see whether the wooden clothespins would taste good. Alice watched her walk across the yard to the back steps.

Like Alice, she wore an old "everyday" dress covered by a large apron. A scarf covered her hair and was tied behind her neck.

Mother stopped beside Alice and looked back at the rugs on the line. "Spring cleaning is a lot of work, but I like the way the house sparkles and shines and smells so good when the cleaning is done."

Isabel and Frank were playing in the grass. Isabel was trying to play house, but Frank didn't understand what he was supposed to be doing. Mother had given Isabel two cracked cups to use in her play. Isabel was trying to have a coffee party with Frank. Alice laughed as she watched Frank stick his nose in the cup, then turn his cup upside down and finally put it on top of his head like a little hat.

Isabel grabbed the cup from his head. "It's coffee, Frank. Don't put it on your head."

Just then Steven came running around the corner of the house. "The mailman is coming down the street."

"Tell you what, Steven," Mother said. "Alice and I need a break. Why don't you get the mail and bring it to the kitchen?"

Alice helped Isabel and Frank wash their hands. Then she took some oatmeal cookies from the crockery cookie jar and placed them on a small plate. She was setting the plate on the table when Steven came in with a couple envelopes.

"There's a letter from Addy." He held it out toward Mother.

"Set it on the table, please, and we'll read it together while we have our snack."

Mother poured milk into pink glasses, and Alice picked up a couple filled glasses to carry to the table.

"I want to help, too." Isabel stood on tiptoe and pulled one of the glasses toward the edge of the counter.

"Hold it!" Alice grabbed the glass before Isabel could spill the milk all over herself and the floor. She handed the glass to Isabel. "Here you go."

Isabel carried it slowly to the table, watching the milk in the glass all the way, as though by watching it she could keep it from spilling.

A bouquet of purple lilacs in the center of the table made the room smell wonderful. The windows beside the kitchen table were open. The breeze coming through them felt good to Alice.

When Mother sat down at the table, she opened Addy's letter. Alice recognized the stationery. "She used the stationery we gave her for Christmas."

Mother smiled. "Why, so she did." While the children helped themselves to cookies, Mother read the letter:

Dear Uncle Donald, Aunt Lydia, Alice, Steven,
Isabel, and Frank,
  Greetings! Thank you for your recent letter and
pictures. I always love hearing from you.

Isabel beamed. "She liked the picture I made her."

Alice squirmed. Isabel had drawn pictures and Steven had written letters to Addy, but Alice hadn't sent Addy anything.

84

Mother continued reading:

This is a beautiful place to enjoy spring. The porch (called the cure porch) looks out over the lake, so the view is lovely. We can watch the squirrels, chipmunks, and rabbits chase busily over the lawn.

After winter's cold weather, the fragrant spring breezes are welcome. I spent many hours along with the other patients on the cure porch even during the coldest days last winter. The nurses saw to it that we were wrapped in rugs and heavy blankets to keep out the worst of the cold. In our rooms, the windows were kept open, even if it was snowing. But that's behind us now.

When I first came, I had to lie flat in bed for a month. That's why I didn't send any letters at first. It was hard to write lying down! The doctors and nurses didn't want me doing anything for myself until my lungs had "had a good rest," as they said. The nurses even insisted on feeding me! I felt rather silly about it all at first, since I felt fine except for my cough and being tired. But Uncle Richard told me it was very important to follow the rules if I want to get better, so I decided I would do just that.

I admit I was lonely for everyone back home at first. I listened to my Christmas radio a lot, and that helped. The nurses kept telling me that cheerful thoughts would help me get better. How could I be cheerful in a strange place when people wouldn't even let me feed myself, I wondered. Finally, I decided to pretend I was a princess, and the nurses were my servants. And who wouldn't want to be a princess?

Mother laughed, and Steven and Alice joined in.

Life is much more pleasant now that I'm allowed to sit up. I've made friends with some other patients my age. We like to play checkers and do jigsaw puzzles together when we're on the cure porch or in the lounge. But we can't play all the time. Every day all the patients nap from two until four.

When I arrived at the sanatorium, I was given a present—a rule book. My friends and I call it "The Book." There is a time for everything at the sanatorium, and a right way to do everything. The Book tells us when to get up, go to bed, eat, brush our teeth, bathe, read. There's a rule for almost anything you can think of! My friends and I spend lots of time making up our own rule book: funny ideas of things we will not *do and when we won't do them—for when we leave the sanatorium, of course.*

Alice gasped softly. How could Addy and her friends make jokes about what would happen to them when they were dead? Mother was still reading:

Tell Alice that every time I look at the sky at night, I think of her beautiful star dance and the words of the Christmas hymn to which she danced. Love certainly did come down with Jesus at Christmas, didn't it? Love came to me at Christmas,

*too, when all of you came to visit me. It comes in
your letters and your prayers, too.*

*Soon Alice and Steven will be out of school for
the summer. What are their plans for vacation?*

With much love,
Addy

Mother folded the letter. "That was nice. After dinner, we
can write to her. But for now, we'd best get back to the spring
cleaning. Alice, will you pack the winter quilts in the cedar
chests? Steven, you can beat the rugs on the line. Beat them
until no more dust comes off them, mind you."

I hope Mother forgets about writing to Addy tonight, Alice
thought while she stuffed a thick quilt into the deep, strongly
scented cedar trunk. *I never know what to say to her.*

But Mother didn't forget. As soon as the dinner dishes
were done and Frank put to bed, Mother called the older children into the kitchen. "I'm going to write to Addy. Each of you
can write a letter or draw a picture for her. I'll mail everything
together so Addy will receive a nice thick envelope to open."

Alice's stomach felt funny. "I. . .I can't right now. I. . .I
have a book I'm supposed to read for school."

Mother looked up from the table where she'd laid out
paper, pencil, and crayons. She shook her head. "Alice, you
always have an excuse for not writing. If it's not homework,
it's that you are too tired or you promised to play with Dot or
Fred."

"I'm going to draw Addy a picture of me and Frank having a tea party," Isabel said, climbing up on one of the chairs.

Steven sat down and reached for a piece of paper and a
pencil. "I'm going to write a letter."

87

"Alice?" Mother raised her eyebrows.

"I have to read my book." She turned and hurried out of the kitchen. It made Alice angry that her mother asked her to write to Addy. She didn't want to write.

Alice found the book she was to read and curled up with it on the velvet-covered sofa in the living room. But she couldn't keep her thoughts on the book. She didn't really need to finish it for a few days anyway.

Her thoughts stayed on Addy. She wished she dared ask someone about Addy, dared ask the questions she really wanted to ask. Did TB hurt? Was Addy in a lot of pain? How long did it take to die? Did dying hurt? But she never heard the adults talk about those kinds of questions, so she didn't dare ask them.

After a while, Alice's stomach growled. She set the book on the sofa cushion and went to the kitchen. Maybe Mother would let her have a cookie. Alice could hear Father and Mother talking when she neared the kitchen.

"I heard something about Alice's friend's father today," Father was saying.

"What friend?" Mother asked.

"That girl Dot, the one whose father used to work for Mr. Foshay."

Alice stopped in the doorway, listening.

"Oh, I hope he found a job!" Mother's voice sounded eager.

"I'm afraid not. He's had to sell his car and his large, beautiful house. He and his family will be moving into a small house in the older part of town. It's a place he's rented out in the past. It will be quite a change for him and his family."

Alice tried to picture Dot in her beautiful dresses leaving her big house and moving into a small old house. She didn't think Dot was going to like moving at all!

CHAPTER 11
Hard Times

"And Father says Dot's family had to sell their beautiful house to pay their bills. They're moving into a house right next to Inez," Alice told Fred on the way to school the next morning.

Fred's eyebrows scrunched together above his blue eyes. "That's too bad."

Alice hugged her books close to her chest. "Dot has always thought she was better than Inez. She even told me and the rest of the girls not to play with Inez. I think it serves her right, losing her beautiful house."

Fred stared at her, wide-eyed. "You don't mean that."

Heat flooded Alice's cheeks. She supposed she shouldn't feel that way about Dot, but she did. "Maybe it will teach Dot a lesson."

"You're always saying Dot should live by the Golden Rule," Fred reminded her.

"She should!"

"Well, what do you think you would do for Dot now if you tried to follow the Golden Rule?"

"Now you're trying to make me feel guilty." Anger made Alice's voice louder than usual.

Fred shrugged. "What you do is up to you. You're the one who's always talking about the Golden Rule."

"Well, I prayed for her father to get a job. Isn't that practicing the Golden Rule?"

"I suppose. But you can't just practice it once and stop, can you?"

For half a block, Alice didn't say anything to Fred. But she didn't like being angry with him. Finally, she said, "Let's talk about something else."

"Yesterday," he said quietly, "a woman sent some bread and rolls she'd made home with Father. Her husband is sick, and Father is taking care of him. Her husband lost his job, like Dot's father, and doesn't have money to pay his bills, so his wife gave Father the bread to pay him for caring for her husband."

Alice didn't know what to say. Surely Dot's family wasn't as poor as this man and woman. After all, Dot's father had made lots of money, and they'd sold that beautiful big house. He must have lots of money left. Hadn't Dot said so when they were making their stars for the Christmas program?

"For a summer project," Fred said, "I was supposed to paint all the screens and storm windows. Now I won't have to.

One of Father's other patients is painting them to pay Father for taking care of his daughter when she was sick."

"You didn't really want to paint them anyway, did you?"

"I guess not," he admitted. "I don't like painting much. But I'll miss the money Father was going to pay me for doing it."

Alice was quiet the rest of the way to school. She'd known there were people who didn't make lots of money, but she'd never known anyone who truly didn't have enough money to pay for things they needed.

When Alice saw her friends talking in the hallway, it was tempting to tell them about Dot. Then she saw Dot's face. She looked sad. *Dot will tell everyone when she wants them to know,* Alice thought. *I guess I shouldn't make her any more unhappy.*

Helping Mother with the dinner dishes that evening, Alice told her about the people who weren't able to pay Uncle Richard for taking care of them.

"A lot of people don't have jobs right now," Mother said. "Sometimes the country goes through a time when there aren't as many jobs as people need. It's hard for people while it lasts, but it always gets better."

"Is it hard for people to get jobs now because of that thing last fall that Father called the stock market crash?" Alice asked.

"That didn't help, but it's probably not the only reason."

Alice set the bowl she'd just wiped on the counter. "Mother, I've been praying for God to give Dot's father a job for a long time. Why doesn't God give him a job? Is Mr. Lane a mean man? Doesn't God want him to have a job?"

Mother seemed to think about the answer for a minute. "I don't know Mr. Lane very well, so I don't know whether he's

91

a mean man. But whether he is a mean man or not, God loves Mr. Lane and his family. Because we don't see God's answers to our prayers doesn't mean God isn't working on them."

"You mean, maybe He's fixing a job for Mr. Lane right now?"

"Maybe." Mother slid her arm around Alice's shoulder and gave her a quick hug. "Let's keep praying for the Lanes. Even if we don't see the answers to our prayers, praying for people is a way of sending them our love."

That night when Alice slipped into bed and said her prayers, a funny picture came into her mind: an envelope with a heart drawn on it was flying through the air with a pair of white wings.

Alice smiled and snuggled down. It made her feel warm and good inside to think she was sending love to Dot and the other people she'd prayed for.

CHAPTER 12

Where's Frank?

Fred grunted as he and his twenty-one-year-old brother, Larry, set the bushel basket filled with orange tomatoes on Alice's back porch.

"That's the last of them," Larry said. He dropped down on the wooden steps.

Fred dropped down beside him. He lifted his hat and wiped the sweat from his forehead with the back of his hand. "Sure hot today."

"It's supposed to be hot. It's August." Larry grinned at him.

"Did you go to the university for three years to learn that?" Fred teased back.

The laughter left Larry's brown eyes. He pushed back the

93

strawberry-blond hair that was so like Fred's. "Hope I can go back this fall."

Fred darted him a sharp look. "What do you mean? Why wouldn't you go back?"

"You know how tight money is these days. The job I've had every summer for the last three years was given to someone else. Not that I'm complaining," Larry hurried to say. "It was given to a man with a family to support. He needed the job more than I did, and he won't be leaving it to go to school this fall. Still, I could use the cash."

"I thought Father was paying for you to go to the university."

Larry leaned back with his elbows on the top step and stretched his long legs out in front of him. "He is, mostly. In the past, I made enough money from my summer job to pay for my clothes and for things like movies and a dinner at a restaurant. Father paid the tuition and books."

"That's what I thought."

"But with so many patients that can't pay their bills to Father in cash, things will be different this year. Father says all the money I've made at odd jobs this summer will probably have to go to help pay my tuition."

Fred knew what Larry meant when he spoke of the patients who didn't pay in cash. The last few months, more and more patients sent things home with Father or came to do some work on the house to pay off their bills. About the only chores left for Fred were the most boring ones, like hauling ashes from the woodstove used to heat the laundry water in the basement and working in the garden.

More and more men were losing their jobs as the bad times grew worse. People kept saying better times were just around the corner, but Fred wasn't sure what corner they were talking about.

Fred chuckled. "Last night when I asked Mother what was for dinner, she said, 'I don't know. Let's see what your father brings home from the office.' "

Larry laughed. "Well, the muffins and sweet corn did taste good."

"And Mom will can the tomatoes today," Fred said.

Larry shook his head. "No one could eat as many tomatoes as we get at our house." It seemed every night Father brought home more tomatoes. And they had tomatoes from their own garden, too.

Both boys jumped when the screen door behind them slammed. It was only Alice.

"You two look lazy. Don't you want to come inside and help can tomatoes?" She grinned at them.

Larry shook his head hard. "Not a chance! That work is way too hot."

"That's for sure!" Fred agreed.

Alice sat down beside Fred. "I think so, too. At first when Mother told me I could help her and Aunt Frances can vegetables from our gardens, I thought it would be fun. It's just hard work. Instead of helping with the canning today, I'm going to watch Isabel and Frank. Dot's going to help me."

Fred looked at her in surprise. "Dot?"

Alice nodded. "At church last weekend, Mother told Dot's mother that she was going to be canning this week. Dot's mother wants to learn how, so Mother invited her to help."

"With three women canning, your kitchen is going to be full," Larry said.

Alice looked over her shoulder at the baskets of tomatoes lined up on the porch. Flies and bees buzzed about them. "I've never seen so many tomatoes."

"Neither have we," Fred agreed. "We were just talking about how many patients are paying Father with things like tomatoes instead of money."

"Father says we need to spend less money," Alice told them.

"Are they laying off men at the mill?" Larry asked.

Alice shook her head. "No. Father says they won't lay anyone off with the summer harvest coming in. But they didn't hire as many men this summer as usual. Instead, men are working longer hours. Father thinks when harvest is over, the mill might lay men off or cut their wages."

Dot and her mother came around the corner of the house, and Alice and the boys jumped up to greet them.

The boys followed Alice, Dot, and Dot's mother into the kitchen, carrying a basket of the tomatoes. Then they left to go home and work in their garden.

"Let's take Isabel and Fred outside and play on the porch or in the shade," Alice suggested to Dot. "It's hot out, but it will be hotter in the house when they're canning."

Dot had brought along a doll, so Alice brought down her doll, Isabel's doll, and an old doll of hers that Frank had taken a liking to.

The corner of the front porch was a perfect place to set up house. A two-foot-high railing made it feel like a house but let in a cool breeze. The girls used an orange crate set on end as a cupboard for their dishes. They pretended the top of the orange crate was their stove. Over the years, Mother had given Alice and Isabel cracked dishes, an old dented kettle, and a couple spoons to use. Another orange crate set upside down made their table.

At first, everyone played well together. Dot and Alice both

wanted to be the mother. They finally agreed both would be a mother. But try as they might to explain to Isabel that she had to be the little girl because she was youngest, Isabel refused. "I'm a mommy," she insisted.

Dot and Alice gave up trying to convince her.

Alice took the dented kettle out and set it on top of the cupboard/orange crate. "I'm going to make dinner. Why don't you set the table, Dot? You can watch our babies, Isabel."

"Don't you have something to use as a tablecloth?" Dot asked.

Alice shook her head. "No. We just use the table like it is."

"It will be much prettier with a tablecloth. I'm going to ask your mother for something to use."

Before Alice could stop her, Dot had headed toward the kitchen. "We aren't supposed to be pestering our mothers while they're canning," Alice grumbled. She couldn't follow and leave Frank alone with Isabel on the porch, so she kept stirring her make-believe stew instead.

By the time Dot came back, Alice was trying to stop Isabel from taking Frank's doll.

"I'm s'posed to watch the babies," Isabel shouted, tugging at one of the doll's legs.

Frank was clutching the doll's head for all he was worth and repeating two of the few words he knew well. "No! Mine!"

Alice was unsuccessfully trying to unwrap Isabel's fingers. "Let Frank play with his doll if he wants to."

"But *I'm* s'posed to take care of the babies," Isabel repeated. She grunted, tugging harder at the doll's leg.

"You're going to pull that leg right out," Alice told her.

Dot knelt beside Isabel. "I know. Why don't you make Frank your helper? Four babies are a lot to take care of for one person. Anyway, you deserve a helper, don't you think, Isabel?"

To Alice's surprise, Isabel let go of Frank's doll right away. Frank clutched his doll tight to his chest.

"Okay." Isabel squatted down in front of him with a hand on each of her knees. "You can be my helper, Frankie. You take care of this baby, okay?"

Frank just glared at her. "Mine."

"Let's put the babies in their blankets," Isabel said. She examined each of the small, worn blankets they had for the dolls, then handed one to Frank. He immediately put one end in his mouth.

Isabel gave a big sigh. "No, Frankie. It's for your baby. Wrap it like this." She took one of the other blankets and sat down in front of him to show him with her own doll.

"That was a good idea, telling Isabel to make him her helper," Alice told Dot as they went back to the orange crates.

Dot held up a white dishtowel with an embroidered basket and flowers on each end. "Look what your mother gave us for our tablecloth."

When Dot laid it over the orange crate, Alice had to admit the table looked much nicer.

"No, Frankie!"

Alice and Dot whirled around to see what Isabel was upset about now. Frank had already pulled the blanket off his doll. Now he was trying to poke one of his pudgy fingers into the doll's eyes. Isabel was pulling at his wrist, and Frank was getting mad.

Alice hurried over. "Stop it, Isabel. If you make him mad, he'll start crying."

"But he's my helper, and he's not doing what I told him."

Alice looked at Dot and rolled her eyes.

Dot held out her hand toward Isabel. "Would you show me

how to set the table right, Isabel? I've never set the table at your house before."

Isabel forgot Frank right away and took Dot's hand.

Alice watched in amazement as Isabel happily took each of the dishes from Dot and showed her where to put it on the table. "Isabel must really like you," Alice told Dot a little later when Isabel was back fussing with the dolls. "She doesn't want to do anything I tell her to do, but she does anything you ask."

Dot shrugged and smiled. "I like little ones. I wish I had brothers and sisters."

"They're a pain sometimes," Alice told her, "but I like them anyway." It was hard for Alice to imagine what it must be like to be an only child. She wondered if Dot got lonely sometimes with no one to play with at home.

The four children took the babies for a walk around the block after their pretend dinner. They only had one baby carriage, so they put two dolls in it and two in Steven's wagon.

Alice thought the walk took a long time. Frank couldn't walk very well, so he had to ride in the wagon with the dolls. Alice and Dot took turns pulling the wagon. Without warning, Frank would decide to get out. If he wanted to walk, Alice or Dot would hold his hand while he took a few slow steps. A few times, he sat down in the middle of the sidewalk to watch a ladybug or try to pull a bit of grass out from between sidewalk cracks. Alice would get impatient and want to put him back in the wagon. Dot would just smile and let him play.

When they got back from the walk, Frank took one of the doll's blankets, curled up in a corner of the porch, and fell asleep. Isabel laid the dolls out for naps, then laid down beside them and fell asleep, too.

While they slept, Mother let the girls make lemonade, enough for themselves and for their mothers, who were hot and sweaty from canning tomatoes.

After squeezing the lemons, they mixed the sugar, lemon juice, and water together. Then they chipped ice from the block of ice in the ice chest and put the ice in large glasses. It made a satisfying cracking sound when they poured the lemonade over it.

The girls carried glasses of the yellow lemonade to their mothers. The kitchen was hot and steamy, even though all the windows were open. There were large bowls of tomatoes on the table and counters. A tall steel thing that looked like a kettle with a heavy cover was on the worktable near the stove.

Mother, Mrs. Lane, and Aunt Frances all wore large aprons that covered their everyday house dresses. Their faces were red from the heat, and their hair was damp from sweat. Alice was glad she wasn't helping with that hard work.

"This is wonderful!" Mother said after she'd taken a long swallow of lemonade.

Mrs. Lane smiled at them. "It's the best lemonade I've ever had."

Alice and Dot beamed at each other.

"Where are Frank and Isabel?" Mother asked.

"Napping," Alice told her.

"Do you have enough lemonade to give them when they awaken?" Mother asked.

"Yes."

"We'd probably better get back and check on them," Dot said.

Alice didn't mind leaving the hot kitchen behind. When they got back to the porch, Isabel and the dolls were lying where they'd left them, but Frank was gone.

CHAPTER 13

Setting a Record

Alice and Dot glanced at each other, then both hurried down the front steps. "He couldn't have gone far," Alice said. Still, her heart beat fast. She could see at a glance that he wasn't in the front yard or in any of the neighbors' yards. And he wasn't on the sidewalk.

"At least he's not in the street." She breathed a sigh of relief. "But where could he have gone?"

"I'll look in the house," Dot said. "You check the yards at

the side and back of the house." She was gone before Alice had a chance to answer.

Alice hurried around the corner of the yard. Guilt and fear spun through her. She always had strict orders to never leave Frank alone. *If anything happens to him, it will be my fault.*

He wasn't along the side of the house, nor in the grass, nor under the spirea bushes that grew beneath the windows. She began running toward the backyard.

It took only a glance to see he wasn't on the back porch or under the maple tree near the house where he and Isabel liked to play. She started toward the garage beside the alley. Steven and some of his friends were playing there with their hoops and sticks, laughing and calling to each other.

Alice's heart felt instantly lighter. Frank must have seen the boys. He was probably sitting in the alley on the other side of the garage, watching the boys play.

She hurried past the garage.

"Hey! Watch where you're goin'!" One of Steven's pals scowled at her as his hoop ran into her.

"Sorry." She pushed the hoop away and slipped around the corner of the garage.

There sat Frank, playing in a small mud puddle in the middle of the weeds behind the garage.

Relief washed away the worry that had filled Alice only moments earlier. She knelt beside Frank, shaking her head. He and his clothes were covered with mud. "What are you doing, sitting in a mud puddle, Frankie?"

He grinned up at her, his tiny teeth sparkling. "Washin'."

He pulled a fist up from the bottom of the puddle and opened it to reveal a stone.

"You're washing *stones?*"

Alice heard a giggle behind her. She looked up. Dot was standing there. "I think we need to wash *him,* don't you?" she asked Alice.

Alice made a face. She didn't feel like giving her brother a bath, but he needed one. She'd have to rinse out his clothes, too.

Dot took Frank's muddy hand. "Let's go play in some other water, okay?"

Frank got up right away. "Okay."

Dot looked over at Alice. "Why don't we ask your mother if we can use a washtub in the backyard to clean him up? That way we won't get her bathroom dirty. Besides," she grinned, "maybe it will cool us off a bit, too."

Alice shook her head as she went to ask her mother for a washtub. Dot sure was different away from school and their friends. Why couldn't she be this nice all the time?

Fred wrapped on the back screen door at Alice's house. Without waiting for someone to answer, he let himself in. He knew he was always welcome at the Harringtons', the same as Alice was always welcome at his house.

Alice and Aunt Lydia were in the kitchen, cleaning up from their Saturday noon meal. Aunt Lydia was singing, as she so often did when she was working about the house. Today she was singing "Let Your Smile Be Your Umbrella."

When they saw Fred come in, Aunt Lydia and Alice welcomed him with warm hellos.

He leaned against the counter and watched them work. "Did you hear the news about June Kelly?" he asked.

Alice shook her head.

Aunt Lydia tilted her head and looked like she was trying to remember. "Isn't June a friend of Addy's?"

"Yes, that's the one." Fred grinned. "So you haven't heard?"

"Heard what?" Alice asked.

"She's trying to break the record for sitting in a tree longer than anyone else."

Alice's eyes grew large. "Really?"

Fred nodded, pleased with her reaction.

"Good for her!" Aunt Lydia started to clap her hands. Soap suds flew everywhere.

Fred and Alice laughed at her, and Aunt Lydia sheepishly joined in.

Aunt Lydia went back to washing the dishes. "I think it's great that a Minneapolis girl is trying something like that."

"She'll have to sit in the tree for many days and nights, won't she?" Alice's forehead puckered in a frown.

"She sure will," Fred agreed.

Alice shook her head. "I don't see how anyone can do that. What if she falls out of the tree while she's asleep?"

Fred shrugged. "Let's go see her and ask. She might be glad for the company. She's probably bored, anyway, sitting up in a tree."

"Would you like to take her some cookies?" Aunt Lydia asked. "I have a copy of last month's *Liberty* magazine, too, if you'd like to take it. June may be glad for something to read."

"That's a great idea." Fred grinned. "You wouldn't by any chance have a couple extra cookies for us?"

"Oh, I think I might be able to spare one or two more."

By the time the two cousins were ready to go, Steven and Isabel had heard of the trip and asked to go along. The four of them had a fun time walking to June's house, which was quite a few blocks away.

All of them were excited to see June in the tree. They often heard on the news about people trying to break records by doing fun or silly things, but they'd never seen anyone try.

"At least sitting in a tree must be easier than trying to win a record sitting on top of a flag pole!" Fred said as they turned the corner to the block where June lived.

They knew right away which tree she was in. Other children crowded around the trunk, staring up at the leaves and talking.

Fred broke into a jog, eager to see June perched in the tree. Alice and the others ran after him.

When they reached the tree, Fred started laughing. He pointed up. "There's the reason she doesn't fall out of the tree when she's asleep, Alice."

In a fork of the large tree, much higher than the house, was a small wooden platform. June sat upon it, her back leaning against the tree.

"It still doesn't look very safe," Alice told him. "It's awfully high. And it's much too small for her to lie down. She must have to sit up all the time."

Fred grabbed hold of a rope that hung from the platform almost to the ground. "Maybe she ties herself to the tree before she goes to sleep." He felt someone yank at his shorts and glanced down.

Isabel was staring up at June. Her brown eyes were huge. "Why is that girl in the tree?"

Fred chuckled. He and Alice had told Isabel three times on the way over why June was in the tree. *I guess she's too young to understand,* he thought. "She just likes sitting in trees, Isabel."

"Oh."

Fred grinned at Alice over Isabel's brown curls. "That was a lot easier than answering half a dozen why's."

"Can I go up there?" Isabel asked.

"No." Alice said firmly.

"Why?"

"Because it's high and it's dangerous," Alice told her.

Isabel pointed at June. "Why is she up there?"

Alice rolled her eyes at Fred, who was laughing again. "She can sit up there if she wants to, because she's big and her Mother and Father said she can sit up there."

"Oh."

When some of the other children had left, Fred waved and called, "Hi, June. I'm Fred Allerton, and these are my cousins, Alice, Steven, and Isabel. Addy Moe is our cousin, too."

"Hi!" June smiled down at them over the edge of her platform. "I think I saw you with Addy at the Foshay Tower last summer. I haven't heard from Addy since she went away. Is she okay?"

"She's still at the sanatorium." Fred lifted a tin box high so she could see it. "We have some cookies for you."

"And a magazine." Alice held it up.

"How kind of you to bring them," June said. "People have been so nice to me since I started this."

"I think everyone in Minneapolis would want you to break the record," Alice told her. "It's awfully brave of you to sit up there."

"Thank you."

Fred looked at the tree trunk carefully. He didn't think he could climb up it. *June must have used a ladder to get up,* he thought. "How do we get the cookies and magazine up to you?"

"There's a basket at the bottom of the tree. Tie the rope to the basket handle, and I'll pull it up," June instructed.

Fred and Alice did as she said.

Fred was surprised when the basket began rising. The rope

wasn't tied to the tree up by June as he'd thought. Instead it was thrown over a thick branch. June pulled on the end opposite the end where he'd tied the basket.

"That's pretty slick," he called up to her. "Like a pulley!"

"It works pretty well," June agreed as the basket reached her perch.

Fred saw her remove the tin box of cookies and the magazine. "This is great! I haven't read this magazine yet. It will be a nice way to pass the time. It does get boring up here sometimes. And the tin box will keep bugs away from the cookies."

June lowered the basket to the ground again.

Isabel ran right over to it. "I want to ride!" She tried to sit in it. "Oof! It's too tight!"

Alice dashed over and pulled her out. "You mustn't sit in there! You'll break it. It's not made strong enough for little girls."

Fred could tell Alice was embarrassed. Her face was fiery red. But he couldn't help laughing. Steven and June were laughing, too. Fred checked the basket. "She didn't hurt it."

Isabel turned to him eagerly. "Can I ride?"

He shook his head. "Afraid not."

She stuck out her bottom lip in a pout.

He always hated to see his cute little cousin upset. "Tell you what. You can't ride in the basket, but you can ride on my shoulders on the way home."

Her face brightened. "Okay."

They talked for a few more minutes with June. Then other friends of June's came by, so they left.

"Thanks for coming!" June called. "Say hello to Addy for me!"

That evening, Alice was excited to see a picture in the newspaper of June on her tree perch. "This is the girl we went to see, Mother."

"So that's Addy's friend." Mother looked from the picture to Alice. "Why don't you send it to Addy and tell her about your visit with June? I'm sure Addy would love to hear about it."

Alice felt the scary sad feelings that always came when her mother mentioned writing to Addy. Alice didn't know what to say. What if she said the wrong thing and made Addy feel more sad? Just thinking about Addy made Alice sad.

She looked down at the picture in the newspaper. June had told them to say hello to Addy for her. She could write about June. That shouldn't make Addy sad. "Okay. I think I will write her."

"Great. You can use some of my stationery if you like."

"All right!" Mother had pretty, nice-smelling stationery. She'd never let Alice use it before.

"I'll get it for you. Why don't you find the scissors and cut out the picture?" Mother headed for her bedroom, where she kept her stationery.

An hour later, Alice sat at the kitchen table staring down at the letter she'd written. She'd told Addy everything she could remember about their visit to June. She'd even told her about Isabel trying to ride in the basket. It was a long letter, but she felt like she should say something else. What?

I wish she wasn't sick. Angry tears blurred the letter. Addy couldn't stop being sick just because Alice didn't want her to be sick.

She sniffed and wiped the tears away with her handkerchief. Her heart hurt as she wrote, "I miss you a lot. I love you. Alice."

A couple weeks later, Alice hurried up the steps to school. The first day back! She could hardly wait to see the friends she hadn't seen all summer.

It would be fun to see Dot again, too. She hadn't seen her since the day their mothers canned tomatoes together.

She spotted her group of friends near the library door and hurried to join them, smiling and saying hello to other friends along the way.

One of the first things she did was show her friends a picture of June from the newspaper. All the girls had read about June. They were excited that Alice had met her.

"It would have been fun to go with you to meet her," Dot said. The other girls agreed.

"I like your jumper, Alice," said Eva, a girl with a narrow face and lots of freckles. "That plaid is so popular."

"Thanks." A warm, happy feeling spread through Alice's chest. It was nice to have her friends notice her new dress. She'd only been able to buy a couple, since their family was trying to save money. But Mother was making her a couple more.

Most of the girls were wearing new dresses, as they usually did the first day of school. She was surprised to see Dot wasn't wearing a new one. The green dress with the drop waist was pretty, but it wasn't new. It was a little too short, too, for Dot had grown over the summer.

Alice noticed Dot shifted her feet uncomfortably and looked away when the girls complimented each other's dresses. *Doesn't her father have enough money to buy Dot a new school dress?* she wondered.

When Dot and her mother were at Alice's to can tomatoes, Dot's father still hadn't found a job. Alice knew that he would go to the grocery store a few minutes before closing on Saturdays and buy things like bananas that wouldn't keep over

Sunday when the store was closed. He could buy them for less than he would have had to pay earlier in the day. Then he would stand on street corners with the things he bought in baskets or boxes and sell them for a penny or two more each than he'd paid.

I wonder if any of our other friends know about Dot's father. Alice glanced at each of their faces. She couldn't imagine Dot telling any of them about her father.

"I think we should all try to talk our fathers into sending us to boarding schools."

Eva's comment jerked Alice's attention away from her thoughts about Dot's father. "What did you say, Eva?"

"Boarding school. Wouldn't it be great if we all went to boarding school together?"

"But. . .why?" Alice didn't think it sounded so great.

"Because we wouldn't have to go to school with all these weird kids."

Alice was confused. "Which weird kids?"

Eva looked at Alice like she couldn't believe Alice didn't understand. "The ones who aren't like us, of course."

"Hi." Inez stopped beside Dot and smiled across at Alice.

Alice smiled back. "Hi. Did you just get here?"

"Yes." Inez turned to Dot, still smiling. "I thought we were going to walk to school together. Did you forget?"

Dot's face grew red. "You must have made a mistake." She turned her back on Inez and started talking to Judy, who was standing on the other side of her.

Shock whipped through Alice. Dot had been mean to Inez in the past, but not this mean. She was so surprised, she just stared. She couldn't think of a thing to say.

Inez tapped Dot on the shoulder.

Dot turned back to her, rolling her eyes. "Now what?"

Inez's brown eyes were calm and sad beneath her thick brown bangs. "I guess I'm good enough to play with when you don't have anyone else, but not when your other friends are around. You only played with me this summer because we live next door to each other, didn't you?"

Dot's face grew redder. "Don't be silly."

"Wait a minute." Eva looked from Dot to Inez. "Did you move into one of those pretty houses by Dot's house?"

Inez shook her head. "No. Dot moved into the house next to mine."

Eva's mouth dropped open. She stared at Dot.

The bell rang, announcing only five minutes left until class. Dot lifted one hand. "See you later, everyone." She was off like a shot, leaving the rest of them behind.

Alice and Inez walked together to their classroom. They didn't talk. Alice didn't know what to say. She didn't know what to think. *Dot had been so nice this summer. How could she turn snobbish again, just because school had started?*

CHAPTER 14
Inez's Secret

"You should have seen Dot's face when Inez told everyone that Dot had moved next door to her," Alice told Fred on the way home from school. "Dot's face was as red as. . .as the red in my jumper."

Fred swung his books in their book strap as the two of them walked along. "What did the other kids say?"

"They didn't have a chance to say anything. The bell rang for classes, and Dot left in a rush. But I could tell by their faces that it was news to the other girls. They all know the poor neighborhood where Inez lives."

"Poor Dot."

Alice stomped her foot. The new shoes made a satisfying smack against the sidewalk. "Fred Allerton, you always stand up for Dot!"

He shrugged and spread his hands. "I feel sorry for her."

"How can you feel sorry for her when she was so mean to Inez?"

"Just because she wasn't nice to Inez doesn't mean her feelings can't be hurt. Things are pretty rough for Dot right now. Think how we'd feel if our fathers lost their jobs and we had to move."

"At lunch, Eva said she didn't think any of us should be friends with Dot anymore."

"Why? Because now she doesn't live in a nice house and wear the best clothes in school? That's pretty dumb."

When he put it that way, Alice had to admit, it did sound dumb. *Still, he should understand that Dot deserves to be treated mean.* "She was mean to Inez. That's a good reason to stop being friends with her."

"Are they going to stop being friends with Inez, too?" he asked.

"Well, most of them aren't very good friends with Inez, anyway."

Fred stopped and stared right into Alice's eyes. She stared back, surprised.

"Alice Harrington, are you going to stop being friends with Dot, like the rest of those silly girls?"

"Ooh, you make me so mad. They aren't silly."

"You didn't answer my question."

"I don't know." Alice hugged her books to her chest and started walking again. "I haven't decided."

Fred caught up to her. "I think Dot needs a friend now more than ever. If Jesus can forgive us for making mistakes and give us another chance, we should be able to forgive Dot, too."

Guilt edged away some of Alice's anger. It made her feel uncomfortable. "I think you should mind your own business, Fred."

Over the next couple weeks, most of the girls in Alice's group of friends stopped spending time with Dot. They'd look the other way when they saw her coming. They'd ignore her if she stopped beside them. If she asked one of them a question, they would usually answer her, but that was as friendly as they would get.

Eva was the one who talked the rest of the girls into treating Dot like she didn't exist. Alice was the only one in the group who was halfway nice to Dot, and she wasn't as nice as she used to be. She couldn't ignore her like the others. She had tried, but each time she did, she felt guilty.

Alice sighed. She was getting tired of feeling guilty.

I'm getting tired of being split between two friends, too, she thought, seeing Inez in the hall ahead of her after school. She hurried to catch up to her. "Wait, Inez!"

Inez kept walking, but she was walking slowly. It only took a minute for Alice to catch up to her. "Didn't you hear me?" Alice asked.

Inez sniffed and brushed the palm of one hand quickly over her cheek. She was clutching her books in front of her and staring at the floor while she walked.

"What's wrong?" *Has Dot said something mean to her again?* Alice wondered.

Inez just kept crying. Alice walked beside her down the hall, out the double doors, and down the steps to the sidewalk. Inez dug a handkerchief from her skirt pocket with one hand and tried to wipe her face. It wasn't easy with her books in the other hand.

Finally Alice took her books. "Why don't I hold these for a minute, so you can blow your nose?"

Alice didn't like seeing her friend cry. It made her own chest hurt. *Why is it always so hard to know what to say and do when someone else is hurting?*

Other students saw Inez crying, too. They just glanced at her curiously and kept going.

When Inez finally stopped crying and was only giving an occasional shaky sniffle, Alice asked again, "What's wrong?"

"It's. . .it's Mom. She's sick."

Alice didn't like it when her mother was sick, either. It felt strange when your mother was sick. After all, she was the one who was supposed to look after the rest of the family when they were sick! But she didn't remember ever crying because her mother was sick.

"Does she have the flu or something?" Alice asked.

Inez shook her head. "Something lots worse. She has TB."

Alice felt frozen and hot and scared all at the same time. It was awful that her cousin Addy had TB, but she couldn't imagine what it would be like if Mother had that terrible disease!

"The. . ." Inez sniffled. "The doctor says Mother has to go to a sanatorium, and I won't even be able to visit her."

"I'm. . .I'm sorry, Inez." *Was that what I should have said?* Alice wondered. She didn't even know what to say to Addy. How could she know what to say to Inez? "I'm sorry," she repeated. She couldn't think of anything else to say.

She saw Fred standing at the corner. "I've got to go. Fred's waiting for me. Here are your books." She took a couple steps then turned back. "I. . .I wish your mother wasn't sick." Then she hurried to meet Fred, wanting to leave Inez's unhappiness behind.

It wasn't as easy to forget Inez and her mother as Alice would have liked. The next day, Saturday, she received a letter from Addy.

On Sunday, the Allertons and Harringtons went to Lake Harriet for a picnic after church. They had a wonderful picnic lunch. After that, they took canoes out on the lake. When they were through canoeing, they had cake. Then the adults visited while the children played.

Alice didn't feel like playing. Instead, she laid in the grass near the edge of the lake, just thinking. A large tree shaded her from the sun.

Fred dropped down beside her. "Hi! What are you thinking about?"

"Addy. I had a letter from her yesterday."

"What did she say?"

"That she was glad I'd sent her the newspaper picture of her friend up in the tree." She'd said Alice's letter had brightened her day, Alice remembered. It left a warm, happy feeling in Alice's heart that her letter had made Addy happier.

"I can't wait until we can sell Christmas Seals again," Fred said. "I wish we could sell them all year long."

Alice laughed. "Then they wouldn't be called Christmas Seals. They'd be called All Year Seals."

"Fred, come here," Steven called from down the shore. "Let's see who can skip stones the farthest."

116

"Be right there!" Fred stood up. "Want to try skipping stones with us?"

Alice shook her head. "I'm happy just lying here being lazy."

When Fred left, Alice closed her eyes. It was nice to lie there and listen to the sound of the water lapping at the shore and smell the grass and the slightly fishy scent from the lake and listen to the birds and the insects.

She heard her mother and Aunt Frances talking and opened her eyes. The women were walking along the shore.

"I'd like to find a job," Aunt Frances was saying. "It would help if we had more cash to pay for Larry's university expenses." She sighed. "I don't suppose Richard would want me to work outside the home, though, even though Fred and Harry are old enough that they don't truly need me about all the time."

"I understand how you feel," Alice's mother said. "I think it would make it easier at our house if I had a job, too. I could always go back to nursing again. Donald thinks the mill may cut workers' hours or lay off workers before long, like so many other companies are doing. We aren't having any trouble paying our bills, but we are trying to save money in case he is laid off."

Father might lose his job? Worry wiggled through Alice's chest. She tried to hold her breath and lie very still so she could hear Mother and Aunt Frances better.

"Why, Lydia," Frances was saying, "surely you wouldn't want to work outside the home when you have four children at home! And soon you'll have another baby to care for."

A baby! Surprise jolted through Alice. She'd noticed her mother's stomach was getting bigger, but she'd thought she was only getting fatter. But then parents didn't usually tell their children about new babies until the baby was born. She sat up, staring after her mother and Aunt Frances.

"Yes and only a couple months before the baby will be here," she heard Mother say.

The women had walked on too far for Alice to hear more. She laid back down, staring at the sky through the leaves. *A baby! I wonder if it will be a girl or a boy.*

Uncle Richard sat down beside her. His straw hat was sitting on top of his black and gray hair at a tilt. He hooked his elbows around his knees and winked at her. "If you're going to lie around beside a lake, you could at least throw in a line. Maybe you'd catch some fish for dinner."

She grinned. "You're not fishing, so why should I?"

"You're right. It's enough to just look at the lake on a pretty day like this." He took off his hat and laid back with his hands behind his head.

Alice couldn't stop thinking about Addy. Last year when the Bell Ringer came to school, her friends had said that people with TB were sent to sanatoriums to die. But Addy was still alive. How long did it take to die?

She sneaked a look at Uncle Richard. *He would know. He's a doctor. I could ask him, right now.* But she didn't. She just thought about it, tried to think of what words she would use. Would he get mad if she asked him? She didn't think people were supposed to talk about dying. Still, everyone knew Addy was going to die. If it was a secret, Addy wouldn't have been sent to the sanatorium.

Alice cleared her throat. "Uncle Richard?"

"Hmmm?" He didn't open his eyes.

"Can I ask you something?"

"Sure." He still didn't open his eyes.

"I mean, something important."

He opened his eyes and looked at her. "Of course, Alice. You can ask me anything you want. What is it?"

"Well. . ." Her hands felt sweaty. She wiped them on her skirt. Then she picked a three-leaf clover from beside her and whirled it between her hands. Now that she had Uncle Richard's attention, she didn't dare ask the question.

"I promise not to laugh or scold," Uncle Richard said quietly.

"Um. . .It's about Addy." She looked at him out of the corner of her eye.

"Yes?"

"How long. . ." She took a deep breath and said as fast as she could, "How long before Addy dies?"

"What?" Uncle Richard sat up as fast as though someone had thrown a pail of water from the lake on him. "What did you say?"

Alice's hands shook. Now she was more scared than ever. "I. . .I said—"

"I heard what you said." He took a deep breath. "It's okay. I told you that you could ask me anything, and I meant it. Who told you Addy was going to die?"

"The girls at school. They said that people with TB are sent to sanatoriums to die."

Uncle Richard took Alice's hand. "Let me tell you a little bit about TB. It's a very dangerous disease. Doctors don't know too much about it. We don't know what causes it. Many people who catch the disease die, but not everyone."

"Even at the sanatorium?"

"Especially there. Sanatoriums are places patients can go where there is clean air and they can rest without needing to go to their jobs or school or take care of their families. I can't guarantee that Addy won't die, but I didn't send her there to die. I sent her there so she could rest her lungs and give them every chance to heal."

"How long will it take for Addy to be well?"

"We don't know. It always takes a long time, though. At least two years. Often it takes five years or more."

"But she could still die."

"Yes, Alice, she could. But she could live for a long time, too."

It seemed strange to think that Addy could live. Alice had been waiting for her to die for such a long time!

"You know, Alice," Uncle Richard continued, "scientists and doctors are trying to find the cause and the cure for TB."

She nodded. "That's why we sell Christmas Seals."

"That's right. Tell me, what else did the girls at school say about TB?"

Alice bit her bottom lip and tried to remember. "Bad things. Dot said people who get TB are filthy." Even thinking about it made her mad. "I told her it wasn't true."

"Filthy?" Uncle Richard rubbed his chin and looked like he was thinking about what Alice said. "I think your friend didn't understand something she was told or overheard about TB. People who live in poor neighborhoods, especially very poor neighborhoods, are more likely to catch TB than people who don't. If people are very poor, they don't have as much money to keep themselves and their places clean. They often live in crowded places instead of big houses with lots of fresh air. Maybe that's why your friend thinks people who get TB are filthy."

"Addy isn't filthy."

"That's right. Your friend is mistaken. People don't have to be filthy to catch TB. Anyone can catch it. What else have your friends said about TB?"

"They said doctors take patients' ribs and that makes patients look funny for the rest of their lives."

"Doctors only take out people's ribs if they think it will help the patient."

"You won't have to take out Addy's ribs, will you?"

"Right now there's no plan to take out Addy's ribs. But if it's the only thing the doctors at the sanatorium think will help her feel better, don't you think they should do it?"

"I suppose so. But I don't think Addy would like it."

"I think Addy wants to feel better."

"I guess so. I wrote a letter to Addy a couple weeks ago. She wrote back and told me that my letter made her feel better."

Uncle Richard smiled at her. "I'm sure it did. Patients at the sanatorium love getting letters. The days can get long and boring there."

Alice sighed. "Sometimes I hurt inside because Addy is sick and I can't help her."

"I feel bad, too, when people are hurting," Uncle Richard said. "That's why I became a doctor. When I'm trying to help them, I don't hurt as bad inside. But even people who aren't doctors can help people feel better, like you did when you sent that letter to Addy."

"Do you think so?"

He nodded. "I do. You know, Alice, your aunt Frances and I are very glad you're our niece. One of the things we like best about you is that you are such a sensitive person."

Alice picked at the clover beside her. "Some people tell me I'm too sensitive. They say my feelings are hurt too easily."

"I don't think that's a bad thing. It means you know how other people feel when they are hurt. That makes you try to treat other people nicely and want to help them when they are hurt, the way you want to make Addy feel better."

"It made me feel better, too, when I wrote to her. I wrote a story for school last week. The teacher said it was good. Do you think Addy would like to read it?"

"I'm sure she would."

Alice twirled a piece of clover between her fingers. A smile stretched across her face. *Maybe I'll write Addy another letter and send her my story.*

CHAPTER 15

A New Baby

A few days later, Alice watched Inez from two rows away in their classroom. *She looks awfully sad,* Alice thought. *I wonder if her mother went to the sanatorium yet?*

Just wondering about it made her chest feel tight. She looked back at the history lesson the class was supposed to be reading. She couldn't keep her attention on it. Her thoughts kept going to Inez.

After class, she waited for Inez in the hall. "Want to eat lunch together?"

"Okay."

They walked together in silence to the cafeteria. Alice wanted to ask about Inez's mother but thought Inez might not want to talk about her in the crowded hall.

Alice picked a table without many people sitting at it. She and Inez sat at one end, near a wall, where Alice knew not many students liked to sit. But even when they were alone, it was hard to ask Inez about her mother.

I wish pretending could make it so her mother wasn't sick, Alice thought. Yet talking to Uncle Richard and writing letters to Addy had made her feel better about Addy. Maybe she'd feel better about Inez if she talked to her. Alice took her roast beef sandwich and an apple out of the tin box she always carried her lunch in.

What should I say? How should I start? Inez hadn't said a word since they'd met after class. *Maybe she doesn't want to talk about her mother or anything else.*

"Do you. . .do you want to be alone today, Inez?"

Inez turned surprised eyes toward her. "No."

"I just wondered because you're so quiet. Sometimes when I'm quiet, I want to be left alone to think about things."

Inez gave her a little smile. "I'm glad you asked me to have lunch with you. I think I'm quiet today because I'm tired."

Alice played with the stem of her apple, looking at it instead of at Inez. "Did your mother go to the sanatorium yet?"

"Yes. She went on Saturday." Inez's voice sounded like she was trying not to cry.

Alice put a hand on her shoulder. "I didn't mean to make you sad."

"It doesn't make me sad to talk about her. It makes me sad that she's sick and not at home."

"My cousin Addy Moe has TB."

Inez looked at her in surprise. "She does?"

Alice nodded. "Everyone in my family and Fred's family

had to take a skin test to see if we had TB, too. It was scary. Addy was the only one with it, though. Did you have to take a skin test, too?"

Inez nodded. "The doctor told us yesterday that no one else in our family has it. He said with Mother at the sanatorium, we probably won't catch it. But I still wish she was home." Inez brushed away the tears that glistened on her lashes.

"I know. I miss Addy, too."

"I'm afraid I won't ever see her again," Inez said in a very soft voice.

"When Addy went to the sanatorium, I thought she was going to die right away. But she didn't. Last Sunday, Uncle Richard told me Addy might not die from TB ever."

Inez's eyes opened wide. "Really? I thought everyone who went to the sanatoriums died."

"That's what I thought, too. Uncle Richard says it's not true. He's a doctor, so he should know." Alice told Inez everything she could remember that Uncle Richard had told her about TB.

"Uncle Richard says the people at the sanatoriums really like to get letters. Maybe if you write to your mother, it will cheer her up."

"I think I'll do that."

"Addy wrote us letters telling what it's like at the sanatorium. If you want, I'll ask Mother if you can read them. Then you'll know what it's like where your mother is."

Inez's face brightened. "Oh, I'd like that!"

The bell blared, reminding the students they had only five minutes to get to class. Alice and Inez stood up, gathering their things together.

Inez smiled at Alice. "It's nice to have someone to talk to about Mother. Most of the kids don't want me to talk about her."

"You can talk to me about her any time you want to."

Alice felt good as they walked back to class together. *It wasn't nearly as scary to talk about Inez's mother and Addy as I thought it would be.* She glanced at Inez out of the corner of her eye. *She looks happier than she did earlier. Maybe I helped her feel better. I hope so.*

The sadness Alice had felt for her friend wasn't as bad as it had been before. A warm joy filled her at the thought that maybe she'd helped her friend feel better.

Almost a month later, in October, Alice's father woke her up one morning.

Alice blinked at him in surprise. "Where's Mother?" Mother was always the one who made sure she and Steven were out of bed each morning so they could get to school on time.

"I took her to the hospital a couple hours ago."

"Hospital?" Alice sat up fast. "Is she sick?"

Father put his hands gently on her shoulders. "Mother is fine. She's going to have a baby."

Happy excitement filled Alice. "The baby is coming today?"

Father nodded. He looked very tired, but he was smiling. "Think you can help me out this morning?"

"Sure. How?"

"If you'll make breakfast for Steven and Isabel, I'll get Frank up and dressed."

It was fun to play Mother and make breakfast, even though it took Alice longer than it took Mother. When they were almost through eating, Father said, "Steven, I want you to help Alice do the dishes. Then I want you both to pack a bag with all the clothes you'll need for the rest of the week."

Alice stared at him in surprise, her glass of milk halfway

to her mouth. "Why? We aren't going away with Mother in the hospital, are we?"

"Mother will be in the hospital for five days or so," Father answered.

"Why so long?" Fear began to wind through Alice. "It doesn't take that long to have a baby, does it?"

Father laughed. "No, it doesn't, but Mother will need to rest after the baby is born. There's nothing wrong with Mother. That's what all new mothers do."

"Oh." Alice's fear slid away.

"Why do we have to pack?" Steven asked.

Father pulled a bowl away from Frank, who was trying to turn it upside down on his head. "Since Mother isn't going to be home for a while, you children will be staying with Aunt Frances and Uncle Richard."

Alice and Steven grinned at each other.

"When do we get to see the baby?" Alice asked.

"It isn't born yet. After you and Steven leave for school, I'll take Isabel and Frank to the Allertons. Then I'll go back to the hospital so I can be there when the baby is born."

"But we want to see the baby, too!" Alice said.

"I want to see the baby!" Isabel pounded a spoon on the tabletop.

Everyone ignored Isabel. Alice didn't think Isabel understood there was going to be a new baby in their house in a few days.

"When the baby is born, either I or Uncle Richard will call and let Aunt Frances know," Father assured them. "The doctors and nurses at the hospital won't allow you children to visit Mother and the baby. That's a hospital rule. But we'll tell you all about it."

Alice's shoulders drooped. It would be hard to wait!

127

"Will you stay at Aunt Frances and Uncle Richard's with us?" Steven asked Father.

"I'll be there for dinner every evening. During the days, I'll have to go to work as usual. I'll probably sleep here at home. I don't know if they have enough extra beds for all of you children and me, as well!"

It was hard to pay attention at school that day. Alice kept watching the clock, trying to make the hands move faster just by wishing. She kept wondering, *Has Mother had the baby yet? Is it a girl or a boy?*

Alice told all her friends about the baby that was coming.

"I'm so jealous!" Dot told her. "I wish I could have a baby brother or sister."

"You'd make a good big sister," Alice said, remembering how nice Dot had been to Isabel and Frank.

Alice and Steven and Fred ran as much of the way from school to the Allertons' as they could. It was cold out and the cold air hurt Alice's nose when she ran, but that didn't stop her.

When Alice got a stitch in her side from running, she had to walk instead. The boys quit running to walk with her, but Steven kept saying, "Can't you walk a little faster?"

"I'm walking as fast as I can!" she said, and she was.

They hurried into the house, dropping their schoolbooks and lunch tins on the hall table. The welcoming smell of fresh baked cinnamon and oatmeal cookies filled the air coming from the kitchen. Without waiting to take off their coats, the children headed for the kitchen.

Isabel was sitting at the kitchen table. Frank was on the floor, playing with some spoons. Aunt Frances was taking a sheet of cookies from the oven.

Alice couldn't wait for Aunt Frances to finish what she was

doing. She had to know right away! "Is the baby born yet?"

Aunt Frances grinned and set the cookie sheet down to cool. "Yes, it is!"

Alice grabbed Steven's hands. "We have a new baby!" They grinned at each other and danced in a circle.

Isabel tried to stop them so she could join in. "I want to dance, too!"

Alice picked up Frank. Steven and Fred each took one of Isabel's hands. They all skipped in a big circle around the kitchen table while Aunt Frances laughed at them.

When they stopped, Alice asked, "Is it a boy or a girl?"

Aunt Frances gave them a mysterious smile. "I'm not telling. You'll have to wait until your father comes for dinner to find out."

"Please tell us, Aunt Frances!" Alice begged.

"Please," Steven said.

Their aunt just shook her head and kept smiling. "That is your father's surprise."

"But I can't wait," Alice wailed. "I feel like I'm going to burst, I want to know so bad!"

Aunt Frances started placing warm cookies on a pretty china plate. "Why don't all of you sit down and have some cookies and milk? Then if you'd like, I'll get some paper and pencils and crayons, and you can each make your mother a card."

"All right," Alice said, setting Frank down on a kitchen chair. "But I still wish you'd tell us whether the baby is a boy or a girl."

"Yes," Steven agreed. "It sounds funny to keep calling it 'the baby' and 'it.' "

Making the cards did help the time go by faster. Alice made two of them, one for Mother and one for the baby. She was just finishing the card to the baby when Father came in.

Alice dashed for him, not giving him a chance to take off his coat. She threw her arms around his waist. "Father! What is it, Father?"

"Is it a girl or a boy?" Steven asked, throwing his arms about Father, too.

Alice couldn't remember ever seeing Father grin so wide. His dark eyes twinkled. "It's a girl."

Alice started jumping up and down. "We have a new sister!"

Isabel squirmed in between Alice and Father. "I want a hug, too."

Father lifted her up and gave her a bear hug. "You're not our littlest girl anymore, Isabel."

"What is our new sister's name?" Alice asked.

"Audrey."

"What does she look like?" Steven asked.

Father laughed. "Like most babies: wrinkled and pink and tiny."

"I'll bet she's pretty," Alice said.

"That she is," Father said in a soft voice. "She has lots of hair for a new baby—dark, wavy hair."

"We made cards for Mother and the baby—I mean for Audrey." Alice picked up the two she'd made. "Will you take them to Mother when you go see her?"

"Of course. She'll love them."

Alice showed him her cards. He read the one to Mother first, then he picked up the one to Audrey. "Dear Baby," he read out loud, "Welcome to our family."

He handed back the cards, then touched his hand to Alice's cheek. "That's a great card."

Alice couldn't stop smiling, and she couldn't wait to see her new baby sister!

CHAPTER 16

A Letter from Addy

During dinner, the children had lots of questions about the new baby, but Father wasn't able to answer most of them. Finally they couldn't think of anything else to ask, and people at the table began talking about other things.

"This early cold wave isn't such a good thing for all the homeless men," Uncle Richard said.

"That's for sure," Alice's father agreed. "I hear a thousand men are staying at the Union City Mission every night, and that's only one of the places homeless men can find a place to sleep inside."

Homeless men was a term Alice heard a lot these days. It always sent a mixture of sadness and fear running through her. *Homeless men has such a lonely sound,* she thought.

"Why don't the men live at home?" Steven asked.

"They don't have homes," his father explained.

Steven shrugged and held up his hands. "Then where do they live?"

"Outside," Fred answered. "Under bridges. In parks. On the streets. Some have managed to build little shacks from old wood or scrap metal or boxes. When it's cold out like it is now, it isn't safe for them to sleep outside. That's why the city has a place they can stay overnight, but they have to leave in the morning. Some Christian organizations have places for men to sleep at night, too."

Steven's blue eyes grew large. "Why don't the men have homes to live in?"

His father sighed. "Since Black Tuesday—the stock market crash that happened a year ago—thousands of people have lost their jobs. They don't have any money to pay for a place to live."

Alice noticed Fred looking at her and tried not to look worried. Whenever the subject of men losing their jobs came up, she worried about what her mother had said about the mill where Father worked. *Would Father lose his job and their family lose their house?* she wondered.

"Since we're speaking of money, Richard," Aunt Frances said to her husband, "I have something to tell you."

"Yes?" Uncle Richard asked.

"You know I do volunteer work with the League of Women Voters. The husband of one of the League women has an opening for a secretary in his law office. The woman suggested I apply for the position."

Uncle Richard almost spit out the milk he'd been drinking. Fred smothered a laugh with his hand.

Father laughed out loud.

Uncle Richard shot Father a dirty glance, then looked back at Aunt Frances. "Why would the woman suggest *you* for the job?"

"Because she thinks I'd be good at it. After all, I've worked with the League for a long time and with Women's Suffrage groups before that. I've lots of experience organizing events and volunteering in the League offices."

"But. . .but. . ." Uncle Richard looked as though he couldn't believe his ears. "But why would you want a job? You don't need to work outside the home."

"I'd be paid. I could help pay for Larry's university expenses or whatever else we need," she said. "After all, with so many of your patients paying you in groceries and by helping out around the house and yard, a little extra cash would be helpful, don't you think?"

Fred, Father, and all the Harrington children turned their faces from Aunt Frances to Uncle Richard.

"Frances, a woman's place is at home, taking care of her children and the house." Uncle Richard was beginning to look upset, Alice thought.

Everyone looked back at Aunt Frances.

She smiled sweetly at Uncle Richard. "Fred is ten. He doesn't need me at home while he's in school. I already spend hours every week doing volunteer work for the League of Women Voters and helping with church work. What is the difference to Fred and our house if I'm working for free or working at a job?"

Everyone looked back at Uncle Richard.

"How would you get all the work around the house done if you were working at a job?"

Everyone looked toward Aunt Frances again. *This is like a tennis match,* Alice thought, trying not to laugh.

"With so many of your patients offering to clean the house and do the mending and laundry and ironing, I've certainly time to work at a job."

Everyone looked back at Uncle Richard.

He threw his hands up. "I give up! If you want to apply for the job, I won't try to stop you. But I must say, I can't understand why you would choose to do so when you can stay home all day instead."

"I only want to feel useful, Richard," Aunt Frances said quietly. "If I can be of more help to our family working at an outside job, then that is what I would like to do."

Alice's father cleared his throat. "Well, I expect my youngsters will keep you busy until Lydia and Audrey come home from the hospital."

Aunt Frances laughed. "Land sakes, they certainly will. I'm not used to having a house full of children anymore. It's lovely having them here."

Alice and Inez walked partway home after school the next day. Alice chattered away about Audrey and what fun it was going to be to have a new baby sister. Finally she realized that Inez wasn't saying very much.

"Is something wrong?" she asked. Then she remembered. "Are you thinking about your mother?"

"Some," Inez admitted.

"Did you want to talk about her?" Alice would rather talk about Audrey, but if it would make Inez feel better, she would listen.

Inez shook her head. "No."

"You look sad."

"I'm tired. Since Mother went to the sanatorium, I've had to do the housework and grocery shopping and cooking and mending. Sometimes, I don't have time to get my homework done anymore."

"I'm sorry." Alice tried to imagine doing all the work her mother did around the house and taking care of the family. She couldn't.

Inez gave her a little smile. "At least I don't have younger brothers and sisters like you do to take care of. I'm the youngest, and my brother is five years older than me. But I wouldn't mind having a baby sister, like you do, even if she would mean more work."

"Maybe when Audrey is a little older, I can take her to visit you."

Inez laughed. "We're already planning her visits, and you haven't even seen her yet."

Alice had to laugh at herself, too.

"Would you like to stop at my house for a few minutes?" Inez asked.

Alice hesitated. She should probably go straight home to the Allertons, but she had a feeling Inez was lonely. "Okay."

"Which house does Dot live in?" she asked as they went up the front steps to Inez's home. She hadn't been to Inez's house for a long time, and she'd never been to Dot's home— at least, not to the house she lived in now. She'd been to parties at the other house Dot lived in. That house had been fancy and very big. Not like the houses on this block.

Inez pointed to a small, single-story house beside her own two-story wooden house.

Inside, Inez had just hung up their coats in the hall closet when there was a knock at the door. Alice wandered into the living room while Inez answered the door.

"Hi, Dot," Alice heard her say.

What is she doing here? she wondered. Inez had told her that she and Dot hadn't talked since the first day of school, when Dot had snubbed her in front of the other girls. Alice peaked into the hall.

Dot held out a small jar. "My mother told me to give you this." Her voice was stiff. "She's returning the sugar she borrowed from you the other day. She said to say thank you."

"You're welcome." Inez took the jar. "Would. . .would you like to come in for a minute?"

Dot bit her bottom lip and came inside. When Inez had closed the door, Dot blurted out. "I didn't come just to return the sugar. I came to say I'm sorry."

Alice didn't know what to do. She was sure Dot didn't know she was here. She knew she shouldn't listen to other people's private conversations, but it wasn't like she was trying to find out someone else's secret.

"Sorry for what?" Inez asked.

"Well. . ." Dot looked at the floor, where she was making circles with the toe of her shoe. "I. . .I wasn't very nice to you the first day of school."

"No," Inez agreed quietly, "you weren't."

Dot's cheeks grew red. Alice *almost* felt sorry for her.

"I didn't want the other girls to find out my father had lost his money and we don't live in the big house anymore," Dot said in a shaky voice. "I guess I was right, because when they found out, they stopped being friends with me."

"Maybe they weren't very good friends to begin with," Inez said, "if they stopped being friends because of that."

Dot nodded. "I know now that it isn't what we own that makes people like us. It's how we treat others that makes people like us."

Inez smiled. "I think you're right."

"Anyway, I'm sorry I treated you so mean. Even last year at school I treated you mean, but during the summer, when we moved next door, you were nice and played with me."

"That's because you were nice to me last summer."

Alice cleared her throat and stepped into the hall. She lifted one hand. "Hi, Dot. I, um, I was in the living room."

Dot's face flared red again. "I guess you heard what I said."

Alice nodded. She tried to think of something to say to make Dot feel less embarrassed. "I thought what you said was smart."

"Want to have some milk and cookies with us?" Inez asked Dot.

Dot's eyebrows shot up in surprise. Then she smiled and nodded.

Passing the door to the living room, Dot said, "It looks like you're sewing something."

Inez sighed. "I'm trying to make over a dress from last year. It's too short. But everything I try to do to it looks terrible."

"Why don't you show us," Dot said. "Maybe Alice and I can think of something."

Inez led them into the living room. From the open sewing machine table, she lifted a green and black plaid dress. "I thought I could put this piece of black velvet from another old dress on the bottom of it to make it longer, but it just makes it look silly. See?"

She's right, Alice thought. *It does look silly.* "I don't know what else you can do."

137

Dot stood back and looked at the dress. She tilted her head to one side and then the other. "What if you put the black velvet strip at the top of the skirt? That way it would look very fashionable."

Alice frowned. "That would be hard. Inez would have to take the whole skirt off and then sew it back on. And there's all those pleats."

Dot shrugged. "I guess it wasn't a very good idea. I know how I like dresses to look, but I don't know how to sew, except to sew on buttons."

"*I* know how to sew, and I'm good at it." Inez's voice sounded excited, and her eyes were shining. "I think it's a great idea, Dot. It will be a lot of work, like Alice said, but I think I can do it. Thanks!"

She laid the dress down and led the way toward the kitchen. "If you'd like, Dot, I could teach you to sew."

"I'd like that."

Alice smiled. She liked this Dot. *And it's nice not to have to choose between my friends anymore.*

"Having a new baby in the house sure makes for a lot of work," Alice told her mother a week later. She lifted her little sister out of the white wicker bassinet and smiled. "But I guess she's worth it."

Mother laughed. "Well, I should think so. It's hard to believe you were ever that tiny."

Alice slipped her little finger between Audrey's fingers. Audrey's fingers were soft and so small that Alice's finger looked gigantic by comparison. "Hi, Audrey. I love you," she whispered.

Mother jumped up from the low bench in front of her

vanity. "I have something to show you."

Alice watched her go to the closet, take down a large round hat box, and set it on the bed. She opened the box and gently lifted out a tiny sweater of the palest pink that Alice had ever seen.

"This was yours," Mother said softly.

Alice's chest filled with wonder. "It's so dainty. And so small. I can't believe I ever fit into it."

"You did. Since you were born in November, you had lots of cold weather in which to wear it." Mother sat down on the bed. She brushed one hand lightly over the sweater. "I'll never forget the night you were born. It was the night of the first presidential election in which all the women in the United States could vote."

"Are you going to let Audrey wear my sweater?"

Mother shook her head. "Oh, no. I don't want to take a chance on anything happening to it. I plan to keep this forever. It's very special because it belonged to you."

Her words made Alice feel like love surrounded her heart.

Mother put the sweater back in the box and put the box away. Then she brought out a package wrapped in brown paper. "I thought you and I could make some sleepers for Audrey. I found this flannel at Dayton's Department Store." She unwrapped the package and lifted out three pieces of cloth. One was white, one a pale blue, and the last a pale pink.

Alice reached out and touched the pink flannel. "It's about the softest thing I've ever felt."

Mother nodded. "Perfect for a baby's skin, don't you think? Would you like to help me make up the sleepers?"

"Yes. I like to sew."

Alice heard footsteps racing up the steps. A minute later,

Steven burst into the room, panting. "The mail came. There's a letter for you from Addy."

Alice took the envelope. Then she sat down in the rocking chair near the bed, where she could hold her little sister while she read the letter. "Would you like me to read it to you, Mother?"

"That would be nice, if you don't mind sharing."

"I don't mind." She unfolded the letter.

Audrey screwed up her face, stretched and twisted, and started to whimper. Alice patted her lightly. "Everything's all right, little sister." She pushed her toe against the floor to start the chair rocking. Almost right away, Audrey stopped crying.

"I can see Audrey is going to like to have you taking care of her," Mother said, her eyes twinkling.

Alice grinned. "Of course. I'm her big sister." She began reading the letter:

Dear Alice,

It was so nice to receive your letter last month. I'm glad you sent along your funny story. You're a good story teller! I hope you don't mind that I read it to some of my friends. They all laughed at it, as I did. They want you to send us more stories.

Alice looked up. "That was the story I had to write for class the first week of school," she told Mother. "It was about a kitten that liked to hide in baskets and went for a ride that she didn't expect to in one of the baskets. I got the idea from the day when Isabel tried to ride in June's basket."

"I remember that story," Mother said. "Addy and her friends are right. It was good."

Alice beamed at her then went back to the letter.

It's been nice on the cure porch lately. The trees around the lake are beginning to turn their fall colors, so the view is very pretty.

The weather has been cool on the cure porch, but wrapped in warm wool blankets, we don't mind the cold. The nurses have taught us how to wrap the blankets so not a bit of breeze can get through. I probably look as bundled up as your new baby brother or sister will be when you take it outside this winter.

Alice looked at her mother in surprise. "Why, she doesn't know Audrey's been born! I'll have to write her a letter right away and tell her."

"That's an excellent idea," Mother said. "Now why don't you finish reading the news from Addy for me?"

I've made more friends here the last few months. One of my special friends is a nurse named Lily. She used to have TB, but she doesn't any longer. Many of the doctors and nurses here once had TB but are healthy now. Most of them are lovely people, patient and cheerful. I think I might like to be a TB nurse one day, when I've recovered from TB. Maybe that's why God brought me here, so I would know what He wanted me to do with my life.

Write and let me know what you are doing in school. If you have any more stories to send, I'd love to read them!

Love,
Addy

Hope made Alice's heart happy. If all those nurses could get over TB, surely Addy could, too!

Audrey had fallen asleep while Alice rocked and read. Now Alice carried her slowly over to her bassinet and laid her down on her back. For a minute, she stood just watching her new sister. She looked so sweet!

Mother still had the flannel for the baby's sleepers spread out on the bed. Alice picked up a piece of it, holding its softness against her cheek.

"Do you think we could buy some more flannel, Mother? I'd like to make a bed jacket for Addy for Christmas. Do you think she'd like that?"

"I think it's a wonderful idea."

"Maybe I can get some blue satin to stitch around the edges and blue ribbons to tie it at the neck."

"I believe we can manage that."

"I could embroider flowers on it, too." It would be an awfully pretty bed jacket. Alice could see a picture in her mind of Addy wearing it. She'd be smiling.